T0285201

supa ya ramen

supa ya ramen

Ramen Reinvented

Luke Findlay

PAVILION

It all started on a grey Wednesday morning, when I was sitting on a bus heading north out of town. One of my best mates Hannell and I were in Tokyo, and I was about to eat one of the most transformative bowls of food of my life...

It began in Tokyo

We were heading to a ramen shop called Ichifuku, a fairly unremarkable little place on a backstreet of a quiet little suburb just north of Shinjuku. Run by an old woman and her daughter, and specializing in one style, miso, I was instantly hooked. Before this, I had only ever eaten tonkotsu-style ramen, so the next couple of weeks in Japan were spent devouring as many bowls and different styles as possible. We ate everything from the infamous black ramen and a clam shio down a back alley in Osaka to salty seafood chintan topped with raw chicken in Kyoto. We even enjoyed dining at a four-times-gold-medal-winning ramen restaurant specializing in tsukemen back in Tokyo. Tasting all these styles and seeing what young chefs were doing (known as the 'new wave') really opened my eyes to what was possible when it came to ramen and really resonated with my eclectic style of cooking.

Back home

Back in London – and back to my day job – all I could think about was ramen, and how no one was really doing any other styles apart from tonkotsu. I had an idea. Originally I thought I'd do a pop up and mess about with a few bowls I'd loved in Japan; I would feed some people, have a bit of fun and carry on with the day job. However, due to various circumstances (lack of money, venue and equipment), I quickly realized that a pop up wasn't a great idea, so I came upon the idea of hosting a supper club: in my flat, in the kitchen, six people a time, three sittings a night, one style, everyone eating the same bowl. It could be fun, I thought. All I had to do now was convince my flatmates. Luckily, at the time, I had a couple of lovely flatmates – Maria and Tamika – who thought it was a great idea. Little did we know what a monster it would turn into...

The start of the supper club

I started an Instagram account. A few mates followed it and I managed to sell out the first Saturday – the majority of guests being mates and a few quizzical ramen fanatics.

The next couple of weeks carried on in the same vein, but, bizarrely, momentum picked up and picked up quick. Within a couple of weeks the waiting list was nearly a month long! I was not a two-star restaurant in town, I was just a bloke having a bit of fun (for the first six months I was usually six beers deep by the last sitting of the evening). It nearly became a full-time job just to deal with the bookings, so I took it back to doing it on a week-by-week basis, which seemed to create even more of a demand for spaces. At its peak, I had 100 people on the waiting list each week for 18 spaces. Mental!

It soon got to the point where the guests were all strangers; Maria was having to hide her toothbrush and I was having to deep-clean the flat every week. It turned into a four-hour service, which was actually a three-day operation. The flat stunk of eggs on Fridays, as I'd sit in front of the television peeling eggs for Saturday. The kitchen would be out of action from about midday, so I could get ready for the evening, then the flat would be full of strangers from 6:30pm to 10:30pm… and if the last sitting were fun, they'd sometimes stay for afters, so my flatmates would have to just sit in their rooms like some terrible halls of residence. And this went on for nearly a year! I don't know how they put up with it to be honest, and I owe Maria and Tamika the world for that. I love them both dearly and would bury bodies for them, no questions asked.

I served over 700 people in that little flat. I made some lifelong friends, including Toby, who is now my business partner and one of my closest mates. I've always wanted to do my own thing, but when I started cooking professionally 20 years ago, the last thing I thought I'd become known for is ramen. I still think it's unreal to this day.

I knew doing this at the flat had an expiry date, and eventually it was time to pull the plug. Weirdly, I can't remember the last one, have no idea who came or what I cooked. It's a shame because I remember the first one so vividly, probably because it was so bad (apologies if you were there). I chatted with my good mate Joe from Patty&Bun about what to do and he gave me some of the soundest advice I'd ever been given: keep going until the demand is so great you have to do something bigger.

Mortimer House

Next up for me was Mortimer House. A six-week takeover in a swanky spot in town. It was a chance to reach out to a different crowd. I was hooked up by my mate Ianthe. Originally, they wanted me to take over an entire floor, then they mentioned they had a little kitchen with an eight-seater table they used for meetings and corporate breakfasts. This sung to me immediately — I could do what I'd been doing for the last year in town, on my terms. This time it would be eight people a sitting, three sittings a night. Easy, right?

What people don't think about when doing pop ups is the logistics. I've done a fair few pop ups in my time, but none where I've had to do everything: order everything, cook everything, pack everything, load everything up, drive, unload everything, set up, finish off any little bits of prep, set up the table and receive guests. I'd done all this before at my gaff, but for some reason this seemed as if there was a lot more at stake. For the last year I'd been having fun at home, now someone was trusting me with their kitchen, taking my bookings at their reception, showing guests to their seats… I felt like a fraud.

The first week, it all felt a bit awkward, but then I just thought to myself: this is no different to home, just a slightly different crowd and a few more covers each night.

Ianthe had taken a massive punt on me here, so I relaxed into it, put my tunes on and had a beer. The only real difference from before was that there was a meat and a veggie option, which I'd never done at the flat (I'd done veggie weeks, but there had always been only one choice). It was nice to offer a bit of a menu.

In fact, apart from the pain of making everything at home, finding a Zipcar and driving into town every Saturday, I really liked Mortimer House. Next came a slew of pop ups.

Pop up in Pakistan

First up was a pop up in Lahore on the top floor of a clothing shop. When they got in touch, I thought it was a scam. Bizarrely, it wasn't. And after a couple of phone calls and a few emails, I was on a plane to Pakistan. What had my life become?

Zain and Nadira owned the clothes shop and had now built an incredibly slick and very busy restaurant on the top floor. There were about 90 covers booked in every night and my pop up was starting in a day – the pressure was on. The team was a mix of very bright, enthusiastic young culinary students from a local college (who were super keen to learn and soaked up every bit knowledge I had) and a few local chefs from a nearby restaurant (who were keen to know what the hell was going on).

The front of house were equally as nice, but none of them had ever worked in restaurants before; they were all employees of Zain's clothing empire. So we had to train the chefs and front of house in 24 hours and open a restaurant to paying customers, around 80% of whom, I'd say, had never had ramen before. It was a massive task, but we just about pulled it off, and, as the week went on, we went from strength to strength.

Popping up around London

Back to London and straight back into a string of pop ups. The formula was always the same: 100 bowls, first come first served, and once they're gone they're gone. This created real hype and we'd have people queuing a good half hour, sometimes an hour, just to get a bowl. This was bonkers, but it showed me there was a real appetite and a place on the scene for my 'traditionally inauthentic' ramen. People were really getting it.

We popped up at Freddie's lovely little café Snackbar in Dalston, where I ended up snapping a muscle in my leg and spending the rest of the night in hospital. We cooked a roast beef bowl on a Sunday in an old chicken shop in Clerkenwell. We cooked a lamb chintan and cemented the now-legendary fried cabbage and cheese at our mate's Chinese restaurant Lucky & Joy in Clapton. We had an amazing weekend cooking with Leachy at Manteca, including a stonking Parmesan and miso brodo with mortadella croutons. We had a great night cooking with our mates the Fourlegs boys at The Compton, inventing the cheeseburger ramen, which has been on and off menus in various guises ever since.

One of the rowdiest collabs we ever did was with Elliot of Lagom, a mad-talented arsonist (in a good way). He made some incredible soups with all sorts of smoky animal bits, I made the noodles and eggs, and we both did bits for the toppings. We stuck to the usual formula, 100 bowls, first come first served. We thought it would be pretty chilled – it was in a big brewery in Hackney and it had a great bar at the kitchen, which sat about

14 people, so we thought we'd keep it intimate and run it like an actual little ramen bar. Boy, did we get it wrong. Come 6pm it properly booted off, and within about 20 minutes there were about 130 on the waiting list (and we'd failed to mention to the staff that we only had 100 bowls, so they kept taking names). Some people waited up to three hours to get a bowl that night. This was the first pop up that Toby had come to and he turned to me amidst the chaos and said: I'm in, let's do it. He's been my right-hand-man ever since.

Search for a shop

Throughout all this, I was trying to find a shop to put down some roots. I found a tiny shop on Hackney Road with a kitchen the size of Harry Potter's bedroom, but it was a start. We did the place up a little, bought some new equipment, came up with a little menu of pop-up classics and geared up for the official opening on the 20th of March 2020… then suddenly, we were in lockdown and we never opened.

I didn't want to tell this story and talk about the coronavirus pandemic, but here we are. We turned it into a delivery service, which was hard work but it kept us active and actually got us out and about seeing people. Once restrictions started to ease, we decided to have bubble bookings nights: six to eight people in the same bubble coming to have a set menu. This proved really popular and gave us the energy to carry on. We also did a pop up with our pals at Top Cuvée during this time, slinging bowls out of their window. It was an absolute roadblock! There were queues snaking everywhere and the police were called, but luckily no one got into trouble and everyone got fed.

We never did open properly on Hackney Road. The size of the place was getting to me, so we decided to find a proper shop. Toby and I spent weeks trawling the streets looking for somewhere. I used to go past this little Scottish café on Kingsland Road on the bus on my way home and noticed it had been closed for some time. I asked Toby to do some digging (he's like a dog with a bone and he will not stop until he gets what he wants). Within a day, we had a meeting with the landlord and 499 Kingsland Road was ours.

499 Kingsland Road

We begged, borrowed and stole to turn it into a ramen shop. I went to the only place I knew I could find the skillsets for the job: my local, The Gun. In this gem of a pub in Hackney, run by Nick and Hannah, you can get anything, or if you can't, someone in there will know someone who can. There I found Chris, Harry and Jaime, talented builders who took my rough sketch on the back of a cigarette packet and made it exactly how we wanted it.

It's been a rollercoaster ever since. We've had to grow up a bit. I mean we now employ people! I thought I'd never say I was an employer, but I love it, and not in a megalomaniac kind of way – it's nice to create a team of lovely people who all get it and see them forming friendships and hanging out.

We've been incredibly lucky with the support we've got from customers since opening, especially the locals. The community has welcomed us and we count many neighbours as friends who pop in for a chat. After toiling away in other people's kitchens for the last 17 years, it's nice to think that I'll retire working for myself and making my family proud.

how to build a bowl

It's really quick to build a bowl in just a few easy steps. I follow the same rules each time, swapping ingredients in and out as I please. Use the building blocks we've given you as a kind of puzzle to figure out what you want to create, and you'll be able to put together endless combinations of flavours.

1 In a ramen bowl, add your flavoured oil **2** Add the seasoning **3** Add the soup **4** Whisk everything together so it's emulsified **5** Cook the noodles and add to the bowl **6** Mix the noodles with chopsticks so they don't stick together **7** Add your toppings **8** Get your head in there and start slurping – the louder the better!

bowls

This is the easy bit. All the hard work with ramen is in the prep. Throwing bowls together is the fun bit! It's also the super-quick part – your tea will be on the table in about 5 minutes. Make sure the prep is on point and you're laughing. I've described the way we plate-up in the shops, but feel free to do it your way (and, if it looks better than mine, I'm nicking it). Also remember, these recipes are just the way we do them. The idea of this book is to give you the building blocks to create your own bowls, so mix things up – use different soups with different seasonings and toppings. I can't be arsed to do the maths, but there's potentially hundreds of different combinations you can come up with, so enjoy getting creative.

There are loads of different styles of ramen and bowls out there – these are a few of my favourites:

- Mazemen/Mazesoba – a soupless bowl of ramen, served with toppings and a seasoning that you mix yourself at the table.

- Tonkotsu – a fatty style of pork ramen.

- Wontonmen – a style of ramen with stuffed wontons as a garnish.

- Tantanmen – a style of ramen with a spicy minced pork topping derived from the Chinese dish 'dan dan'.

- Chashu – a popular topping, typically a roast or braised cut of pork marinated in soy and spices.

For each bowl, there'll be a few steps that are always the same, so I'll tell you those now. Then, once you've done it a few times, it'll be second nature to you.

- The noodles should always be cooked in unsalted boiling water for 1 minute 10 seconds. Always. Unless you want less of a chew, then you can cook them for longer – just keep testing them until you get the right bite for you. We like them chewy at Supa Ya Towers.

- Always shake off the excess water, cos if you don't, you'll end up diluting the soup, which will make it boring, and no one likes boring soup.

- To warm the egg up, place the egg in a mug, boil some of the marinade and pour it over – simple.

the kimchi double double bowl

Serves 1

(page 110) 1x **fudgy egg** 25g **white cabbage** 25g **cucumber**
50g (page 137) **house kimchi** 25g **beansprouts**
250ml/1 cup (page 93) **confit tomato and garlic soup**
25g **momoya kimchi base** 1 portion **noodles**

1 Warm the egg (see page 15) and bring a pan of unsalted water to the boil. Prepare a pan of cold water next to it, ready for dunking the noodles in.

2 Thinly slice the cabbage and cucumber, and add them to a mixing bowl with the kimchi and beansprouts.

3 Put the kimchi base in a ramen bowl and pour over the soup. Give it a good whisk to mix them together.

4 Cook the noodles in the boiling water for 1 minute 10 seconds (see page 15). As soon as they're cooked, shake off the excess water and plunge them into the cold water. Move them around in the water and kind of give them a little wash with your hands. Once they're cold, add them to the serving bowl.

5 Add the egg to the bowl, then heap on the cold kimchi vegetables.

Served cold, this is good on a hot summer's day – refreshing soup, chewy noodles and crunchy veg with a slight tang from the kimchi.

celeriac chashu and fried garlic bowl

Serves 1

250ml/1 cup (page 96) **roasted vegetable and olive oil soup**

3 slices (page 114) **celeriac chashu with marinade**

1x (page 110) **fudgy egg** 30ml/2 tbsp (page 76) **roast garlic oil**

60g (page 86) **sesame miso** 40g (page 84) **house chilli paste**

1 portion **noodles** 1, green part only, sliced **spring onion** 3 tsp **fried garlic**

large pinch **korean red pepper powder**

1. Bring the soup to the boil, warm the egg (see page 15) and bring a pan of unsalted water to the boil. Warm the celeriac chashu through in a pan with a little of its marinade, which will also give it a nice glaze.

2. In a ramen bowl, combine the garlic oil, sesame miso and chilli paste. Add the soup and give it a good mix to emulsify.

3. Cook the noodles in the boiling water for 1 minute 10 seconds (see page 15). Add the noodles to the bowl and give them a good wiggle with some chopsticks.

4. Add the egg to the right of the noodles (this will give you a guide to where to put the rest of the ingredients).

5. Layer on the celeriac chashu to the left of the bowl. Place the spring onion/ scallion in the middle and sprinkle on the red pepper powder and fried garlic.

One of the big hitters from the supper club days, vegetarian ramen has never been so good! Bore off with your mushroom and tofu bowls.

fried cabbage and cheese bowl

Serves 1

120g Hispi or white **cabbage** 45–60ml/3–4 tbsp **olive oil** Maldon **sea salt**

250ml/1 cup (page 96) **roasted vegetable and olive oil soup**

1x (page 110) **fudgy egg** 30ml/2 tbsp (page 76) **roast garlic oil**

60g (page 86) **sesame miso** 40g (page 84) **house chilli paste**

1 portion **noodles** 5g/2 tsp **fried garlic** generous grating **parmesan**

1 Chop the cabbage into fairly chunky dice. Fry it super-quick in a little olive oil and season well with sea salt. You want to cook it so it still has a little bite to it.

2 Bring the soup to the boil, warm the egg (see page 15) and bring a pan of unsalted water to the boil.

3 In a ramen bowl, combine the garlic oil, sesame miso and house chilli paste. Pour the soup into your bowl and give it a good whisk to emulsify.

4 Cook the noodles in the boiling water for 1 minute 10 seconds (see page 15). Add the noodles to the bowl and give them a good wiggle with some chopsticks.

5 Add the egg to the right of the noodles (this will give you a guide to where to put the rest of the ingredients).

6 Heap the cabbage to the left of the egg. Scatter the fried garlic over the cabbage and heap the Parmesan all over everything – don't be afraid to get heavy-handed with the cheese, you can never have too much cheese!

Is it a bowl of ramen? Is it a bowl of cheesy pasta? Who cares! My all-time favourite – go extra hard on the cheese.

mapo tofu mazesoba

Serves 1

200g (page 109) **mapo tofu** 1x (page 110) **fudgy egg**

30ml/2 tbsp (page 76) **roast garlic oil** 50ml/3½ tbsp (page 83) **house soy**

1 portion **noodles** 1, green part only, sliced **spring onion**

1 Warm the tofu in a pan, warm the egg (see page 15) and bring a pan of unsalted water to the boil.

2 In a ramen bowl, combine the roast garlic oil and house soy. Whisk together to emulsify.

3 Cook the noodles in the boiling water for 1 minute 10 seconds (see page 15). Add the noodles to the bowl and give them a good wiggle with some chopsticks. You need to give them a really good mix so the noodles are all coated.

4 Add the tofu and again give it a really good mix.

5 Place the egg on top and add the spring onion/scallion.

Served sans soup. Mix it all up and it's good to go.

chopped omelette, xo butter and kewpie mayo bowl

Serves 1

3x **eggs** 250ml/1 cup (page 100) **white chicken soup** 60g (page 86) **sesame miso**

40g (page 84) **house chilli paste** 1 portion **noodles**

squeeze **kewpie mayo** 5g/ 2 tsp **fried garlic** 5g/ 2 tsp **fried onions**

1, green part only, sliced **spring onion** a good pinch 3g/ **togarashi** (page 75) **xo butter**

1. Make an omelette out of the eggs. Try and keep it a bit gooey in the middle.

2. Bring the soup to the boil and bring a pan of unsalted water to the boil. Melt the XO butter.

3. In a ramen bowl, combine the miso and chilli paste. Pour the soup into the bowl, giving it a good whisk.

4. Cook the noodles in the boiling water for 1 minute 10 seconds (see page 15). Add the noodles to the bowl and give them a good wiggle with some chopsticks.

5. Roll up the omelette and chop it widthways. Layer the omelette on top of the noodles. Squeeze the mayo over the top of the omelette to your liking, then cover with the fried garlic, fried onions, spring onion and togarashi. Generously douse in XO butter.

This is a great breakfast bowl: hot and spicy, eggy and crunchy. The mayo might sound weird going into a hot bowl, but trust me, it works. I won't give a quantity of the mayo and butter to add, just pile it all on until you're happy.

fried red pepper prawns, crab and yuzu kosho bowl

Serves 1

10g/1 tbsp **korean red pepper powder** 3x **prawns**

150g **white crab meat** juice of 1 **lime**

3g/½ tbsp **black sesame seeds** 5g/2 tsp **yuzu kosho**

75ml/5 tbsp **olive oil** 250ml/1 cup (page 97) **roasted shellfish soup**

30g (page 81) **ginger-infused pork fat** 60g **miso** 1 portion **noodles**

1. Sprinkle the red pepper over the prawns/shrimp and set aside.

2. Put the crab meat in a small bowl and dress it with the lime juice, sesame seeds and yuzu kosho. Set aside.

3. Heat 2 tablespoons of the olive oil in a frying pan and fry the prawns until pink and cooked through. Once cooked, remove from the heat and add the remaining olive oil to the pan. You can use this peppery prawn oil to dress the bowl at the end.

4. Bring the soup to the boil and bring a pan of unsalted water to the boil.

5. In a ramen bowl, combine the pork fat and miso. Pour the soup into the bowl, giving it a good whisk to emulsify.

6. Cook the noodles in the boiling water for 1 minute 10 seconds (see page 15). Add the noodles to the bowl and give them a good wiggle with some chopsticks.

7. Layer the prawns on top and cover with the crab. Drizzle over the prawn oil to finish.

Perfect for the summer, this can be served ice-cold or is just as good hot.

braised octopus, raw asparagus and fermented chilli bowl

Serves 1

250ml/1 cup (page 97) **roasted shellfish soup** 1x (page 110) **fudgy egg**

1x **tomato** 200g (page 116) **braised octopus**

2, thinly sliced **asparagus spears** 10g/2 tsp (page 138) **fermented chillies**

1, green part only, sliced **spring onion** 60g **miso**

30g (page 81) **ginger-infused pork fat** 1 portion **noodles**

1. Bring the soup to the boil, warm the egg (see page 15) and bring a pan of unsalted water to the boil. Deseed the tomato and cut it into 5-mm/¼-in dice.

2. In a small pan combine the octopus, asparagus, chillies, tomato and spring onion/scallion. Add a couple of spoonfuls of the reserved octopus cooking liquor and gently warm through. Don't boil it or heat it for a long time, as you don't want the asparagus to cook — you want that textural difference between the crunchy asparagus and the soft octopus.

3. In a ramen bowl, combine the miso and pork fat. Add the soup and give it a good whisk to emulsify.

4. Cook the noodles in the boiling water for 1 minute 10 seconds (see page 15). Add the noodles to the bowl and give them a good wiggle with some chopsticks.

5. Place the egg to the right of the bowl. Spoon on the octopus mix to the left of the egg, completely covering one side of the bowl.

You can prepare the octopus the day before, then let it rest in its cooking juices overnight to really take up all the flavour.

smoked bacon tonkotsu, roast turbot and caviar bowl

Serves 1

300g **block smoked pancetta** 1 litre/4 cups (page 98) **fish bone soup**

1x (page 110) **fudgy egg** 20g/ 1½ tbsp **unsalted butter**

150g **turbot fillet** 250g **smoked bacon tonkotsu**

30ml/2 tbsp (page 80) **smoked bacon oil** 1 portion **noodles** dollop **caviar**

1 Cut the pancetta into 5-cm/2-in cubes. In a deep pan, sweat off the pancetta until it is nice and dark. Add the soup and bring to the boil. Simmer for about 3 hours, then strain. You should have a nice creamy, bacony soup at this point.

2 Bring a pan of unsalted water to the boil. Warm the egg (see page 15).

3 Heat the butter in a frying pan and cook the turbot in the foaming butter until golden brown and cooked through (put a cocktail stick/toothpick into the thickest part of the fish and then put it to your lip; if it's the same temperature as your lip or hotter, then it's done).

4 Put the smoked bacon oil in a ramen bowl. Pour the soup into the bowl, giving it a good whisk to emulsify.

5 Cook the noodles in the boiling water for 1 minute 10 seconds (see page 15). Add the noodles to the bowl and give them a good wiggle with some chopsticks.

6 Place the egg to the right and the fish in the middle of the bowl. Finish with a healthy dollop of caviar on top of the fish.

For this bowl you'll have to slightly adapt one of the soups, but it's not a major hassle.

seared scallops, smoked pancetta and pickled red chillies bowl

Serves 1

5 slices **smoked pancetta** 15–30ml/ 1–2 tbsp **neutral oil**

3x **scallops** 250ml/1 cup (page 101) **roast chicken wing soup**

60g **miso** 30g (page 81) **ginger-infused pork fat** 1 portion **noodles**

about 20g (page 135) **pickled red chillies** sprinkle **chopped chives**

1. Fry the pancetta in a frying pan with the oil until it is nice and crispy. Remove from the pan and set aside.

2. In the same pan, sear the scallops in the pancetta fat for 2 minutes on each side, or until you get a really good crust on both sides but they are still a little opaque in the middle.

3. Bring the soup to the boil and bring a pan of unsalted water to the boil.

4. In a ramen bowl, combine the miso and pork fat. Pour the soup into the bowl, giving it a good whisk to emulsify.

5. Cook the noodles in the boiling water for 1 minute 10 seconds (see page 15). Add the noodles to the bowl and give them a good wiggle with some chopsticks.

6. Place the scallops at 12, 3 and 9 o'clock, then layer over the pancetta in the gaps. Spoon over the chillies and sprinkle over the chives.

A great little surf and turf bowl, perfect for brunch.

mortadella wontonmen, clams and wild garlic bowl

Serves 1

250ml/1 cup (page 101) **roast chicken wing soup**

1 portion (page 117) **mortadella wontons and clams**

60g **miso** 1 portion **noodles** 1 slice **mortadella**

1 Bring the soup to the boil. Bring a pan of unsalted water to the boil. Cook the wontons in the boiling water until al dente, then remove from the water with a slotted spoon and set aside. Bring the water back to the boil.

2 Add the miso to a ramen bowl. Pour the soup into the bowl, giving it a good whisk to mix together.

3 Cook the noodles in the boiling water for 1 minute 10 seconds (see page 15). Add the noodles to the bowl and give them a good wiggle with some chopsticks.

4 Place the wontons to the left of the bowl and the reserved clams to the right, then drape over the reserved slice of mortadella.

A carb-on-carb delight but it is super light so it feels like you're getting away with it. You can add the cooking juices from the clams, if you like, so you can have a 50/50 soup.

fried chicken and butter-poached lobster bowl

Serves 1

250ml/1 cup (page 97) **roasted shellfish soup** 1x (page 110) **fudgy egg**

30g (page 81) **confit garlic chicken fat** 1 piece (page 120) **boneless fried chicken** 1 portion **noodles** 1, green part only, sliced **spring onion**

butter-poached lobster

1x **lobster tail** 300g/ 2¾ sticks **butter** 2x **garlic cloves** grated zest of ½ **lemon** large pinch **togarashi** 1x **star anise**

1. Start by making the butter-poached lobster. Remove the lobster meat from its shell and set aside. In a small pan, bring 100ml/scant ½ cup water to a simmer. Reduce the heat to very low and whisk in half the butter, making sure it doesn't boil and the butter doesn't separate). Whisk in the remaining butter, then smash the garlic and add it to the pan with the lemon zest, togarashi and star anise. Infuse off the heat for 30 minutes.

2. Add the lobster tail to the pan and very gently poach it over a low heat for 5–6 minutes, turning every minute or so until just cooked. Set the pan aside.

3. Bring the soup to the boil, warm the egg (see page 15) and bring a pan of unsalted water to the boil.

4. Put the chicken fat in a ramen bowl. Add the soup, giving it a good whisk.

5. Cook the noodles in the boiling water for 1 minute 10 seconds (see page 15). Add the noodles to the bowl and give them a good wiggle with some chopsticks.

6. Place the egg to the right of the bowl. Put the fried chicken to the left and the lobster tail on the top. Scatter around the spring onion/scallion.

Another over-the-top bowl! You can use the fried chicken from the snacks section (see page 120) for this recipe.

roast chicken, greens and black truffle bowl

Serves 1

4x leaves **cavolo nero** 1x skin-on **chicken breast** Maldon **sea salt**

30ml/ 2 tbsp **neutral oil** 250ml/1 cup (page 101) **roast chicken wing soup**

1x (page 110) **fudgy egg** 30g (page 81) **confit garlic chicken fat**

50ml/3½ tbsp (page 83) **house soy** 20g **chopped black truffle in oil**

20ml/4 tsp (page 80) **roast chicken oil** 1 portion **noodles**

1 Strip the cavolo nero leaves off their stalks and blanch in salted boiling water until tender. Drain, cool and squeeze out any excess water. Chop and set aside.

2 Season the skin-side of the chicken with sea salt and place a pan over low heat. Add the oil to the pan and cook the chicken skin-side down quite slowly to get the skin really crispy. When the flesh starts turning a little opaque, flip it over and turn off the heat. Let it finish cooking in the pan's residual heat, a lot like you're cooking a piece of fish. Let it rest while you're putting the bowl together.

3 Bring the soup to the boil, warm the egg (see page 15) and bring a pan of unsalted water to the boil.

4 In a ramen bowl, combine the chicken fat, house soy and black truffle. Pour the soup into the bowl, giving it a good whisk to emulsify.

5 Cook the noodles in the boiling water for 1 minute 10 seconds (see page 15). Add the noodles to the bowl and give them a good wiggle with some chopsticks.

6 Place the egg to the right of the bowl. Place the cavolo nero at 12 o'clock. Carve the chicken and place just below the cavolo nero. Drizzle over the roast chicken oil. If you are using fresh truffle, then go for it and shave a load over everything.

You can use an actual black truffle instead. Finely chop some to flavour the soup and shave some over the finished bowl.

roast chicken and corn bowl

Serves 1

1x **chicken breast** Maldon **sea salt** 30ml/ 2 tbsp **neutral oil**

250ml/1 cup (page 101) **roast chicken wing soup** 1x (page 110) **fudgy egg**

60g (page 112) **buttered chilli corn** 30ml/2 tbsp (page 76) **roast garlic oil**

60g (page 86) **sesame miso** 1 portion **noodles** 1, green part only, sliced **spring onion**

5g/ 2 tsp **fried garlic** 1.5g/ pinch **korean red pepper powder**

2.5g/ ½ tbsp **black and white sesame seeds**

1. Season the skin-side of the chicken with sea salt and place a pan over low heat. Add the oil to the pan and cook the chicken skin-side down quite slowly to get the skin really crispy. When the flesh starts turning a little opaque, flip it over and turn off the heat. Let it finish cooking in the pan's residual heat, a lot like you're cooking a piece of fish. Let it rest while you're putting the bowl together.

2. Bring the soup to the boil, warm the egg (see page 15) and warm the buttered chilli corn in a pan. Bring a pan of unsalted water to the boil.

3. In a ramen bowl, combine the garlic oil and the sesame miso. Add the hot soup and whisk to emulsify.

4. Cook the noodles in the boiling water for 1 minute 10 seconds (see page 15). Add the noodles to the bowl and give them a mix up with some chopsticks.

5. Add the egg to the right of the noodles (this will give you a guide to where to put the rest of the ingredients).

6. Slice the chicken and layer it in a fan opposite the egg. Between the chicken and the egg, dollop on the buttered chilli corn. Scatter the spring onion/ scallion, fried garlic, red pepper powder and sesame seeds on top.

Probably our most iconic bowl. Creamy and chickeny, the slightly nostalgic flavour of chicken and mushroom Pot Noodle is an absolute winner.

miso curry butter chicken bowl

Serves 1

3x **chicken breasts** 3x **garlic cloves**

50g **ginger** 200g/¾ cup **natural yogurt**

10g/5 tsp **garam masala** 5g/1 tbsp **ground coriander**

5g/2½ tsp **ground cumin** 5g/1 tbsp **smoked paprika**

5g/2 tsp **ground turmeric** 5g/2 tsp **chilli powder** 100g **miso**

sauce
100g/7 tbsp **butter** 1x **onion** 3x **garlic cloves**

50g **ginger** 10g/5 tsp **garam masala** 10g/2½ tbsp **ground coriander**

10g/5 tsp **ground cumin** 5g/2 tsp **chilli powder**

400g can **chopped tomatoes** 200ml/scant 1 cup **double cream** 50g **miso**

to serve
1 portion **noodles**

1. Start by preparing the chicken. Cut the chicken into bite-size pieces and finely chop the garlic and ginger. Put the chicken in a bowl and add the chopped garlic and ginger, natural/plain yogurt, all the spices and the miso. Mix everything together, cover and leave in the fridge overnight to marinate.

2. Remove the chicken pieces from the marinade.

3. For the sauce, heat the butter in a saucepan, add the chicken and fry it in the hot butter, getting a nice colour all over. Remove from the pan and set aside.

4. Finely chop the onion and garlic, and add them to the pan. Gently fry for a few minutes until softened. Add all the spices and cook slowly for 10 minutes. Add the tomatoes and cook for another 5 minutes.

5. Pour the sauce into a blender or food processor and blitz to a fine purée. Pour the sauce into a clean pan and add the double/heavy cream and miso (check for seasoning, it might take a little more miso). Add the chicken to the sauce and gently tick over until the chicken is cooked through. Cover and leave to rest in the fridge, ideally overnight or for a couple of hours, but if you can't wait, it'll still be good to go straight away.

6. To serve, warm the sauce and cook the noodles in unsalted water for 1 minute 10 seconds (see page 15). Put the noodles in a ramen bowl, pour over the sauce and chicken and give it a good mix. This is also good to eat as a ramen – if you're having it as a ramen, then use the white chicken soup (see page 100).

Messy, rich, buttery nonsense. This is a bit tricky to make for one bowl, so make a batch of it and keep some to eat over rice.

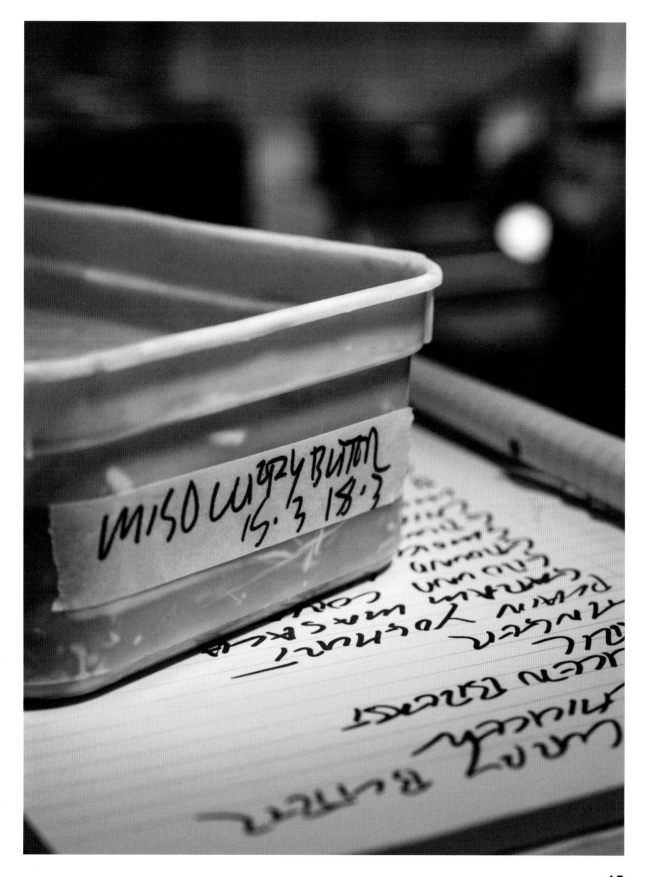

green eggs and ham bowl

Serves 1

1x **egg** Maldon **sea salt** 3–5 slices **serrano or parma ham**

250ml/1 cup (page 101) **roast chicken wing soup**

1 portion **noodles** 150g (page 89) **green sauce**

1 Bring a pan of unsalted water to the boil. Once boiling, add the egg and cook for 6 minutes. Once cooked, refresh in cold water until cool enough to handle, then peel and slice in half. Hit the yolks with a little Maldon sea salt. Set aside.

2 Bring another pan of unsalted water to the boil.

3 In a frying pan, slowly fry the ham to get it crispy (it'll get super-crispy super-quick, so keep an eye on it). Remove and let it drain on some paper towels. You can add the ham fat from the pan into the soup if you want an extra hit of hammy goodness.

4 Bring the soup to the boil, then pour into a ramen bowl.

5 Cook the noodles in the boiling water for 1 minute 10 seconds (see page 15). Once they're cooked add them to the bowl with the soup. Spoon over half the green sauce, layer over the ham and place the egg halves on top. Spoon over the remaining green sauce to finish.

This bowl doesn't have the usual seasonings of soy or miso to add flavour, but uses the green sauce to slowly melt into the soup to season it. Instead of having a fudgy egg with this, it's fun to have an oozy little number, so we'll do a 6-minute egg instead.

ham, egg and chips mazesoba

Serves 1

3 large, peeled **maris piper potatoes**

for deep-frying **sunflower oil** 100g (page 119) **ham hock chashu**

1x (page 110) **fudgy egg** 1 portion **noodles**

40g (page 125) **supa ya pickles** 1, green part only, sliced **spring onion**

mazemen sauce

125ml/ ½ cup **xo sauce** 75ml/5 tbsp (page 83) **house soy**

60ml/4 tbsp (page 80) **smoked bacon oil**

20ml/ 4 tsp **rice wine vinegar**

salt and pepper seasoning

50g **dried whole red chillies** 15g/ 2 tbsp **five spice powder**

25g/ 3½ tbsp **ground white pepper** 50g/ 3½ tbsp **fine salt**

1 First make the mazemen sauce. You can make a big batch of this and it'll keep in the fridge for ages, or reduce the quantities and make just what you need (40g per bowl). In a food processor, blitz everything together until smooth. If you want it a little chunkier, just whisk it all together in a bowl until emulsified. Set aside.

2 Next make the salt and pepper seasoning. Again you can make a big old batch of this and keep it in an airtight container – it'll keep indefinitely.

3 Using a Japanese mandoline or a spiralizer, spiralize the potatoes. Carefully wash them in cold water to get rid of the starch, then pat them dry.

4 Heat the oil for deep-frying in a deep frycr or large pan to 180°C/350°F. Deep-fry the spiralized potatoes until golden brown and super crispy. Once cooked, drain on paper towels, then transfer to a large bowl and hit them with loads of the salt and pepper seasoning. Set aside.

5 Gently warm the ham hock chashu in a pan, warm the egg (see page 15) and bring a pan of unsalted water to the boil.

6 Put 40g of the mazemen sauce in a mixing bowl.

7 Cook the noodles in the boiling water for 1 minute 10 seconds (see page 15). Add the noodles to the bowl and give them a good wiggle with some chopsticks. Make sure all the noodles are coated with the sauce.

8 Transfer the noodles to a ramen bowl along with any remaining sauce. Around the edge of the bowl arrange the ham, pickles, spring onion/scallion, potatoes and egg.

This is a little bit more effort as there's a few bits to make ahead of time. Well worth the effort though. Another soup-less bowl where the different elements are arranged nicely on top – you can nibble on them as they are or go straight in and mix the whole thing up.

slow-roast tomato, bacon, onion and jalapeño hash bowl

Serves 1

250ml/1 cup (page 100) **white chicken soup** 1x (page 110) **fudgy egg**

30ml/2 tbsp (page 80) **smoked bacon oil** 60g (page 86) **sesame miso**

40g (page 84) **house chilli paste** 1 portion **noodles**

slow-roast tomato

1x **beef tomato** Maldon **sea salt**

jalapeño hash

5 slices **smoked streaky bacon**

30ml/ 2 tbsp **neutral oil** 1x **Spanish onion**

2x **garlic cloves** ¼ bunch **coriander** ¼ bunch **chives**

¼ bunch **parsley** 2x **jalapeños**

1 Start by making the slow-roast tomato. Preheat the oven to 120°C fan/ 140°C/275°F/Gas 1.

2 Top and tail the tomato so it has a flat top and bottom. Slice through the equator. Lay the tomato halves on a baking tray and season well with Maldon sea salt. Slow-roast for 2–3 hours – you'll be able to tell when they're done as they will look beautifully roasted with a lovely colour and will have shrunk and tightened up a bit. Cooking the tomatoes this way will intensify the flavour ten-fold and they will be super-tomatoey.

3 To make the jalapeño hash, finely chop the bacon. Heat the oil in a frying pan and sweat off the bacon until really crispy, then transfer to a bowl using a slotted spoon and set aside.

4 Finely chop the onion and garlic, and cook in the bacon fat until nice and soft. Remove from the pan and mix into the bacon.

5 Finely chop the coriander/cilantro, chives, parsley and jalapeños, and add them to the bowl. That's the jalapeño hash done.

6 Bring the soup to the boil, warm the egg (see page 15) and bring a pan of unsalted water to the boil.

7 In a ramen bowl combine the bacon oil, miso and chilli paste. Pour the soup into the bowl, giving it a good whisk.

8 Cook the noodles in the boiling water for 1 minute 10 seconds (see page 15). Add the noodles to the bowl and give them a good wiggle with some chopsticks.

9 Place the egg to the right, add a tomato slice in the middle and spoon a load of the hash over the top of the tomato. You won't need all of the hash or the other tomato slice.

This is a great little brunch number, but it's also a perfect all-rounder.

smoked bacon, morel and truffle mapo tofu bowl

Serves 1

2x **eggs** Maldon **sea salt** (page 118) 200g **smoked bacon, morel and truffle mapo tofu** 60g **miso** 250ml/1 cup (page 101) **roast chicken wing soup** 1 portion **noodles** 1, green part only, sliced **spring onion**

1. Bring a pan of unsalted water to the boil. Once boiling, add the eggs and cook for 6 minutes. Once cooked, refresh in cold water until cool enough to handle, then peel and slice in half. Hit the yolks with a little Maldon sea salt. Set aside.

2. Bring another pan of unsalted water to the boil. Warm the smoked bacon, morel and truffle mapo tofu through gently in a pan.

3. Add the miso to your ramen bowl.

4. Bring the soup to the boil, then pour into the ramen bowl. Whisk the miso into the soup.

5. Cook the noodles in the boiling water for 1 minute 10 seconds (see page 15). Once they're cooked, add them to the bowl with the soup. Spoon over the warm smoked bacon, morel and truffle mapo tofu.

6. Arrange the egg halves on top and scatter over the spring onion/scallion.

Over the top, decadent and daft... but oh so good. If you want to get even more decadent, try swapping the chicken soup for the roasted shellfish soup (see page 97).

carbonara-style mazesoba bowl

Serves 1

3 slices **smoked streaky bacon** 1x **onion** 2x **garlic cloves**

15–30ml/
1–2 tbsp **neutral oil** 1x **egg** 2x **egg yolks**

3g/
¾ tsp **knorr chicken powder** large pinch **cracked black pepper** 1 portion **noodles** grated (optional) **parmesan**

1. Chop the bacon and finely chop the onion and garlic. In a frying pan, sweat off the bacon in the oil. As it starts to colour, add the onion and garlic and fry gently until soft. Allow to cool.

2. In a small bowl, combine the egg, egg yolks, chicken powder and pepper.

3. Once the bacon and onion mixture has cooled down, add it to the eggs.

4. Bring a pan of unsalted water to the boil and cook the noodles in the boiling water for 1 minute 10 seconds (see page 15). Strain the noodles and return to the saucepan.

5. Add the egg mixture to the noodles and stir over very low heat until the egg is just cooked. You can always hit it with more pepper and a load of Parmesan, if you're that way inclined.

All you carbonara purists out there, I said 'style', alright?

spicy black bean sausage bowl

Serves 1

250ml/1 cup (page 101) **roast chicken wing soup** 1x (page 110) **fudgy egg**

15ml/1 tbsp **neutral oil** 3 fat slices (page 122) **black bean sausage**

50ml/3½ tbsp (page 83) **house soy** 40g (page 84) **house chilli paste**

30g (page 81) **ginger-infused pork fat** 1 portion **noodles**

1, green part only, sliced **spring onion**

1. Bring the soup to the boil, warm the egg (see page 15) and bring a pan of unsalted water to the boil.

2. Heat the oil in a pan and fry the sausage until it is nicely crisped up. Set aside.

3. In a ramen bowl, combine the soy, chilli paste and pork fat. Add the soup and give it a good mix to emulsify.

4. Cook the noodles in the boiling water for 1 minute 10 seconds (see page 15). Add the noodles to the bowl and give them a good wiggle with some chopsticks.

5. Place the egg to the right and, following the curve of the bowl, place the sausage opposite.

6. Pile on the spring onion/scallion.

Once the sausage is made, this one is super easy to put together. This sausage is also great just with a couple of fried eggs and some hot sauce for breakfast.

cumberland sausage tantanmen bowl

Serves 1

150g (page 123) **cumberland sausage tantanmen**

250ml/1 cup (page 100) **white chicken soup** (page 110) 1x **fudgy egg**

60g (page 86) **sesame miso** (page 84) 40g **house chilli paste**

1 portion **noodles** 1, green part only, sliced **spring onion**

1. Gently warm the sausage tantanmen topping through in a pan.

2. Bring the soup to the boil, warm the egg (see page 15) and bring a pan of unsalted water to the boil.

3. In a ramen bowl, combine the sesame miso and chilli paste. Add the soup and give it a good mix to emulsify.

4. Cook the noodles in the boiling water for 1 minute 10 seconds (see page 15). Add the noodles to the bowl and give them a good wiggle with some chopsticks.

5. Add the egg to the right of the noodles (this will give you a guide to where to put the rest of the ingredients).

6. Spoon on the sausage topping, then scatter over the sliced spring onion/ scallion.

An absolute must-have for a hangover! Meaty and spicy, this bowl will make you feel brand new again.

smoked pork jowl, crab, and chicken fat bowl

Serves 1

250g **smoked pork** 250ml/1 cup (page 101) **roast chicken wing soup** 30g (page 81) **confit garlic chicken fat** 100g **brown crab meat** 1 portion **noodles** 1, green part only, sliced **spring onion**

1. Bring a pan of unsalted water to the boil. If you have a steamer basket, then place the pork inside it and steam it over the water to heat it up (if not, then very gently warm it through in some chicken stock).

2. In a ramen bowl, combine the chicken fat and crab meat.

3. Bring the soup to the boil, then add it to the bowl and give it a whisk to emulsify.

4. Cook the noodles in the boiling water for 1 minute 10 seconds (see page 15). Add the noodles to the bowl and give them a good wiggle with some chopsticks.

5. Slice the pork and layer it over the noodles. Pile the spring onion/scallion just to the side of the pork.

If you're lucky enough to have a good mate like my pal Shaun Whitmore, then you can go round to his, use his smoker and drink beers in the afternoon sunshine, while he cooks you lunch and you while away the day talking nonsense as the jowls slowly do their thing. If you don't have a Shaun in your life, then go and find a Polish deli, as they do incredible chunks of smoked pork.

cheeseburger mazesoba bowl

Serves 1

25g **aged beef fat** 30g (page 88) **american cheese sauce**
1x **aged beef patty** Maldon **sea salt** 1 portion **noodles**
35g (page 88) **burger sauce** 45g (page 128) **bread and butter pickles**
5g/ 1 tbsp **white sesame seeds**

1. Bring a pan of unsalted water to the boil. Warm the beef fat in a pan until melted, then transfer to a small mixing bowl. Set aside. Warm the cheese sauce and set aside. You can get cheffy and have your cheese sauce and burger sauce in squeezy bottles, if you like.

2. Season the beef patty well with Maldon salt. Heat a frying pan over high heat and sear the patty really hard for a couple of minutes on each side to get a nice crust on the outside while leaving it pink in the middle so it's still nice and juicy inside. Leave it to rest for 5 minutes. Once it's rested, tear the beef patty into bite-size pieces.

3. Cook the noodles in the boiling water for 1 minute 10 seconds (see page 15). Once they're cooked, add them to the beef fat and give them a good mix so all the noodles are coated in the fat.

4. Transfer the noodles to a ramen bowl, scatter the burger pieces on top and squeeze on both sauces. On top of the sauces scatter over the pickles and finish with the sesame seeds.

A cheeky riff on a classic, basically a Big Mac in a bowl. You should be able to get rendered beef fat from a decent butcher if you ask nicely.

spicy sesame shortrib mazesoba bowl

Serves 1

50ml/3½ tbsp **sesame sauce** (page 84) 20g **house chilli paste**

(page 144) 150g **glazed shortrib** (page 135) 30g **pickled red chillies**

1, green part only, sliced **spring onion** 1 portion **noodles**

1 Bring a pan of unsalted water to the boil.

2 In a mixing bowl combine the sesame sauce and the chilli paste, whisking them together until fully combined.

3 Gently warm the shortrib in a small pan.

4 Cook the noodles in the boiling water for 1 minute 10 seconds (see page 15). Add the noodles to the bowl and give them a good wiggle with some chopsticks.

5 Empty everything into a ramen bowl. Cover with the shortrib, pickled red chillies and sliced spring onion/scallion. Tackle it as is or give it a mix up before eating.

Paid-up banger. Spicy, creamy, meaty and finished with some sharp pickled chillies to cut through all that richness.

salt beef and pickles bowl

Serves 1

250ml/1 cup (page 101) **roast chicken wing soup** 1x (page 110) **fudgy egg**

30ml/2 tbsp (page 80) **smoked bacon oil** 40g (page 84) **house chilli paste**

50ml/3½ tbsp (page 83) **house soy** 1 portion **noodles** 3 good slices **salt beef**

40g (page 125) **supa ya pickles** 1, green part only, sliced **spring onion**

2.5g/ ½ tbsp **white sesame seeds**

1 Bring the soup to the boil, warm the egg (see page 15) and bring a pan of unsalted water to the boil.

2 In a ramen bowl, combine the bacon oil, chilli paste and house soy. Add the hot soup and give it a good whisk to emulsify everything.

3 Cook the noodles in the boiling water for 1 minute 10 seconds (see page 15). Add the noodles to the bowl and give them a good wiggle with some chopsticks.

4 Add the egg to the right of the noodles (this will give you a guide to where to put the rest of the ingredients).

5 Layer on the salt beef to the left. Place the pickles in the gap and top with the spring onion/scallion and white sesame seeds.

A nod to the East End and a playful – if not a little messed-up – take on a salt beef bagel. Salt beef can be bought online or found in a well-stocked deli.

'fry up' bowl (the works)

Now this bowl is more of a suggestion than a recipe as everyone has their own version of a fry up. For me, personally, I like to have sausage, bacon, fried eggs, mushroom, tomato, beans, black pudding, bubble and a fried slice. It's entirely up to you how to tackle it, but one thing you should definitely make for it is the buttered toast soup (see page 94), as this brings the whole bowl together.

fridge bingo mazesoba bowl

When I lived with Maria and we were skint or couldn't be bothered to go to the shops, the rallying cry of FRIDGE BINGO echoed out around the flat. There is absolutely no recipe for this, whatever you have in the fridge is fair game. Think of it like an episode of 'Ready Steady Cook' and get creative. We put this on at our last day in Hackney Road to try and get rid of all the food we had left over. We didn't think anyone would order it, but EVERYONE ordered it and we cleared out the fridges. A real fun thing to do. There's no wrong answer.

flavoured oils and fats

Flavoured oils and fats are an integral building block in making a great tasting bowl of ramen. As well as creating flavour, they also replicate that lovely velvety mouthfeel you would usually only get with fattier soups. In Japan, as well as using hot fat in the broth, a lot of the shops will pour it over the finished bowl to help lock in the heat, so the bowl stays hot from the first slurp until the last. We use about 100g per bowl – sounds like a lot, but no one said this was going to be a health food book! Each recipe will make about 20 portions, but kept in an airtight container they'll last for ages.

charcoal oil

Serves 20

fist-sized chunk **lumpwood charcoal** 1 litre/ 4 cups **rapeseed oil**

1 Burn the charcoal for 30 minutes, then cool it a little.

2 Add the oil to a heavy-bottomed saucepan. Carefully add the slightly cooled charcoal, then quickly put the lid on and stand back (if the coal is too hot it can boil the oil and cause it to spatter). Leave it to infuse for an hour.

3 Strain and keep in an airtight container for up to 1 month.

This one is a little trickier, but well worth it as it has such a unique smoky flavour. It can be a little dangerous, so you might want to do it outside or after you've had a barbecue when you have hot coals at your disposal. Use pure lump coals (not briquettes).

xo butter

Serves 20

250g **unsalted butter** 125ml/ ½ cup **xo sauce**

1 Blitz the butter and XO sauce together in a food processor until completely combined. Chill until ready to use.

This is so easy to make and gives you that perfect hint of umami flavour — it's fantastic drizzled over seafood dishes.

roast garlic oil

Serves 20

3x **garlic bulbs** 1 litre/ 4 cups **rapeseed oil**

1 Split the garlic bulbs in half across the equator. Add the oil and garlic to a pan and slowly bring to a simmer. Let it tick over nicely until the garlic becomes a deep golden brown, then take it off the heat and let it cool down.

2 Strain and keep in an airtight container for up to 1 month.

Tip: If you want to make a burnt garlic oil, let the garlic go super dark in the oil, removing it from the heat just before it turns black.

This is always in one bowl or another, so we always have litres of it on hand in the shop.

parmesan oil

Serves 20

250g **parmesan rind** 1 litre/ 4 cups **rapeseed oil**

1 Cut the Parmesan rind into chunks.

2 Add the oil and cheese chunks to a pan and slowly bring to a simmer. Cook it out until the cheese almost looks deep-fried, about an hour.

3 Strain and keep in an airtight container for up to 1 month.

If you use a lot of Parmesan at home, save the rinds for this (always great in braises, ragùs and stews anyway). If not, you can use both the rind and cheese.

seaweed oil

Serves 20

1 litre/4 cups **rapeseed oil** 50g **kombu** 25g **nori**

1 Add the oil and seaweeds to a pan and bring up to a simmer. Simmer for 30 minutes, then take off the heat and allow to steep overnight.

2 Strain and keep in an airtight container for up to 1 month.

This has a great oceany, umami flavour, and can be added into dressings for salads.

anchovy oil

Serves 20

1 litre/4 cups **rapeseed oil** 300g **brown anchovies**

1 Add the oil and anchovies to a pan and slowly bring up to a simmer. Cook out really slowly for about 30 minutes, being very careful not to burn the anchovies as they will turn bitter. Allow to cool and infuse for a couple of hours.

2 Strain and keep in an airtight container for up to 1 month.

Use this oil to add a hint of fish to dishes or combine it with the seaweed oil to get a real taste of the seaside.

shellfish oil

Serves 20

1 litre/4 cups **rapeseed oil** 200g **prawn shells**

2x **garlic cloves** 3g/1¼ tsp **fennel seeds**

3g/1¼ tsp **coriander seeds** 3g/1¼ tsp **annatto seeds**

1 Add half the oil to a pan and heat it until nice and hot. Add the prawn/shrimp shells and fry them nice and hard, smashing them up with a blunt object. They'll turn a lovely deep red and start to release their own oils.

2 Add the garlic and spices and then add the rest of the oil. Bring up to a simmer and let it gently tick over for an hour. Allow to infuse overnight.

3 Strain and keep in an airtight container for up to 1 month.

This one is great to add that sweet seafood taste to your cooking. It looks fantastic and will make the bowl pop.

roast chicken oil

Serves 20

1 litre/4 cups **rapeseed oil** 250g **chicken wings** 5x **garlic cloves** 1x **onion** 1 sprig **fresh thyme** 1 sprig **fresh rosemary** a few **fresh sage leaves**

1 Add 200ml/scant 1 cup of the oil to a pan and get it nice and hot. Chop the chicken wings into 2.5-cm/1-in pieces and add the wing pieces to the hot oil. Pan-roast them until they're a deep golden brown all over.

2 Smash the garlic and roughly chop the onion, then add the garlic and onion to the pan and cook until golden brown. Add the herbs and cover with the rest of the oil. Bring up to barely a simmer and cook for 5 hours, or cover with foil and cook overnight in an oven on 100°C fan/120°C/Gas ½. Allow to cool.

3 Strain and keep in an airtight container for up to 1 month.

Tastes like a roast dinner, what more do you want?

smoked bacon oil

Serves 20

1 litre/4 cups **rapeseed oil** 500g **smoked streaky bacon**

1 Add the oil and bacon to a pan and bring to the boil. Turn the heat down and simmer until the bacon is deep golden brown and crispy. Let it cool down.

2 Strain and keep in an airtight container for up to 1 month.

Another oil we've used since day one. Smoky and meaty, it tastes like the best part of a fry up. Keep the bacon after and put it in a sarnie if you like deep-fried bacon. (Who doesn't?)

ginger-infused pork fat

Serves 20

500g **iberico pork fat** 100g **ginger**

1 Add the fat and the ginger to a pan and place over a low heat. Allow the fat to melt, then slowly simmer the ginger in the fat for 1 hour. Allow to cool.

2 Strain and keep in an airtight container for up to 1 month.

The OG from the supper club days. I use Iberico pork fat for this, which you can find in good butcher shops. It's not cheap but it tastes great. Alternatively, if you don't want to use pork fat, you can swap it out for beef, duck, goose or lamb; it all works.

confit garlic chicken fat

Serves 10

1kg **chicken skin** 20x **garlic cloves**

1 Peel the garlic and put in a medium pan with the chicken skin. Cover with water about 2.5cm/1in above the skin. Really slowly cook out letting it blip away for an hour or so. The water will very slowly evaporate leaving the fat behind.

2 Either strain completely, squeezing all that goodness through a fine chinois, or scoop the garlic out then pass through a chinois, then add the chicken fat and garlic to a blender and blitz until smooth. Chill and eat it like ice cream.

Garlicky chickeny goodness, great just to spread on toast.

These are some of the seasonings we use in our bowls either to build up flavour or to finish the bowl by adding another whack of flavour right at the end so it's the first thing you taste.

house soy

Makes 750ml/3 cups

1x garlic bulb 1 litre/4 cups **soy sauce** 500ml/2 cups **ponzu soy sauce** 150g **ginger** 3x **spring onions**

1. Cut the garlic bulb in half across the middle. Peel and roughly chop the ginger. Roughly chop the spring onions/scallions.

2. Add everything to a pan and cook over medium heat until reduced by half, then allow to cool.

3. Strain and keep in an airtight container for up to 1 month.

house chilli oil

Makes 2 litres/8½ cups

125g **sichuan peppercorns** 125g **preserved black beans** 250g **chilli flakes** 25g **msg** 25g/5 tbsp **smoked paprika** 25g/5 tsp **fine salt** 25g/2 tbsp **caster sugar** 1.5 litres/6¼ cups **rapeseed oil**

1. In a food processor finely blitz the peppercorns, followed by the black beans. Add them to the pan with the rest of the ingredients, making sure everything is covered by the oil. Place the pan over a low heat and, very slowly so it doesn't catch, bring it up to 110°C/225°F, then turn off the heat.

2. Allow to cool, then keep in an airtight container for up to 1 month.

house chilli paste

Makes 1.2 litres/4¾ cups

1 litre/4 cups **gochujang** 100g **aleppo chilli flakes**
100ml/scant ½ cup **rapeseed oil**

1. In a bowl mix everything together until completely combined.

2. Store in an airtight container in the fridge for up to 1 month.

One of the originals, this adds real depth and heat to the bowl.

house chilli crisp

Makes 1.3 litres/5¼ cups

150g **whole dried red chillies** 25g/10 tbsp **sichuan peppercorns** 100g **preserved black beans** 25g/5 tbsp **smoked paprika** 100g **fried garlic** 100g **msg** 25g/2 tbsp **caster sugar** 25g/5 tsp **fine salt** 750ml/3 cups **rapeseed oil**

1. Blitz the dried chillies in a food processor until still quite chunky. Blitz the peppercorns to a fairly fine powder, followed by the black beans. Add all the ingredients except the oil to a pan.

2. In a separate pan, heat the oil to 110°C/225°F. Pour it over the other ingredients, give it a good stir and allow to cool. Keep in an airtight container for up to 1 month.

This is our version of the legendary chilli oil Lao Gan Ma. It is great added to anything you'd use chilli oil on – or in.

sesame miso

Makes 1.3kg/5 cups

1kg **miso** 300g **tahini**

1. Mix the miso and tahini together in a bowl until completely combined.

2. Keep in an airtight container in the fridge for up to 2 weeks.

For this we use a koji miso, which is quite fruity and not overly salty (cheaper miso can be very salty with little depth). I'd recommend trying a few different ones and find one you really like – the finished bowl and your future self will thank me later. The same goes for the tahini, it really is worth finding a good one for that lovely, creamy, nutty finish.

spicy sesame dressing

Makes 1kg/4½ cups

450g **tahini** juice of 2 **lemons** 75ml/⅓ cup **light soy sauce** 150g (page 84) **house chilli paste**

1. Put the tahini and 250ml/1 cup of water into a bowl and whisk together. It will split at first, but keep whisking and it will come together. Whisk in the lemon juice and soy, then whisk in the chilli paste.

2. Keep in an airtight container in the fridge for up to 5 days.

This is great just mixed through some instant noodles for a quick late-night snack.

burger sauce

Makes 550g/2½ cups

3x **gherkins** 300g/ scant 1½ cups **mayonnaise** 150g/ ⅔ cup **tomato ketchup**

100ml/ scant ½ cup **american mustard** 2g/ 1 tsp **paprika**

1 Finely chop the gherkins, then add to a bowl with the rest of the ingredients. Mix everything together until combined.

2 Keep in an airtight container in the fridge for up to 5 days.

Our take on a Big Mac sauce.

american cheese sauce

Makes approx. 500g/2 cups

300g **american cheese slices** 200ml **milk**

1 In a pan warm about 200ml/scant 1 cup of milk up to a simmer. Start adding slices of cheese, whisking as you do. It will take a lot of cheese.

2 You want a kind of squeezy cheese consistency, so keep adding cheese and milk until you have a nice, creamy, squeezable mess.

3 Keep in an airtight container in the fridge for up to 5 days.

There's no real recipe for this, it's more of an eyeball job. You just have to work it until it's the right consistency.

green sauce

Makes 450g/1¾ cups

100g **spring onions** 100g/1 cup **parsley**
15g **brown anchovies** 2x **garlic cloves**
50g/3 tbsp **dijon mustard** 50g **jalapeños**
100ml/scant ½ cup **olive oil** 5g/1 tsp Maldon **sea salt** juice of 1 **lemon**

1 Put all the ingredients in a food processor and blitz until you have lovely smooth sauce.

2 Keep in an airtight container in the fridge for up to 5 days.

This is great added to a meaty bowl at the end to give it a real lift. It's also great with grilled/broiled fish.

Makes 600g/2 cups

400g **red chillies** 100g **scotch bonnet chillies**
as needed **caster sugar** as needed **fine salt**
500g/1¾ cups **runny honey** 5g/1 tsp Maldon **sea salt**

1 Put all the chillies in a food processor and blitz to a fine pulp; stalks, seeds and all.

2 Weigh the pulp and add 2% each of that weight in the sugar and fine salt. Mix together.

3 Transfer to an airtight container and leave at room temperature to ferment for a couple of days, then move to the fridge. This will be your chilli mash.

4 Put 100g of the chilli mash in a pan with the honey and salt. Slowly melt together over a low heat and then allow to gently cook for about 30 minutes.

5 Leave to infuse for another 30 minutes, then strain.

6 Keep in an airtight container in the fridge for up to 1 month.

Great drizzled on salads, meats, anything really. Gives a lovely, balanced hot-sweet finish.

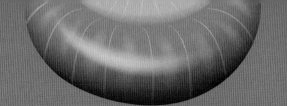

Soup. The backbone of every good bowl of ramen. Lovingly made, taking hours upon hours – sometimes days – of careful prep, skimming, tweaking and temperature adjustments. Some people measure the viscosity of the soup to make sure it has the right mouthfeel. We cheat. Don't get me wrong, I love a stock sitting on the back of the stove blipping away, seeing to its needs every few hours, making sure we're still getting on, but in this day and age people are generally tight on space and time and there's more of an instant (want it now) culture, so we use pressure cookers to make our soups. A soup that would traditionally take 10 hours plus, we can do in about an hour and a half. If you don't have a pressure cooker, then rough timings will be offered for stove-top stocks. Also, don't bother peeling vegetables for soups; waste of everyone's time.

confit tomato and garlic soup

Serves 15

10x **plum tomatoes** Maldon **sea salt** 5x **garlic cloves** big drizzle **olive oil** 100g **kombu**

1. Halve the plum tomatoes and arrange them in a roasting pan, cut-side up. Season each tomato with Maldon sea salt. Thinly slice the garlic and arrange them over the tomatoes. Drizzle with the olive oil to coat. Leave them for an hour or so to let the salt dig in.

2. Preheat the oven to 130°C fan/150°C/300°F/Gas 2.

3. Put the tomatoes in the low oven and cook for about 3–4 hours. They will shrink and intensify in flavour.

4. Transfer the tomatoes to a pressure cooker or pan and add 5 litres/20 cups water. Cook on full pressure for 1 hour, then allow to depressurize naturally. If using a pan on the hob/stovetop, bring up to a boil, then turn down to a simmer and let it simmer for 3 hours.

5. Now add the kombu and let it steep for 30 minutes. At this stage, you can either strain it (so you have a clear broth) or you can take the kombu out and blend the soup (so you have a thicker, creamier soup).

6. Pass through a fine chinois. Serve at once or allow to cool and keep in the fridge for up to 5 days.

A super-light umami-heavy soup, packed full of flavour.

buttered toast soup

Serves 10

1 loaf cheap **white bread** plenty **salted butter**
3 litres/ 12 cups **soup of your choice**

1 Toast the bread – no, reaaalllllly toast it! It needs to be super toasted. Don't be scared if it's a little burnt round the edges. Slather each slice with more butter than you should.

2 Bring the soup to a simmer, then add the toast. Allow to simmer for 30 minutes, then take it off the heat and let it steep for 2 hours.

3 Pass through a fine chinois. Serve at once or allow to cool and keep in the fridge for up to 5 days.

4 When it's cold, the butter will rise to the top and set. When you're reheating it, make sure all the butter is back in the soup and give it a good whisk so every bowl is super buttery. Remember, butter is your friend.

With this soup you can use either of the chicken soups (see pages 100 and 101), veg soup (see page 96) or the tomato soup (see page 93) as a base.

roasted vegetable and olive oil soup

Serves 15

5x **carrots** ½x **leek** 1x **spanish onion**
1x **garlic bulb** 3 sticks **celery** 3x **vine tomatoes**
½x **fennel bulb** big drizzle **olive oil**

1 Preheat the oven to 180°C fan/200°C/400°F/Gas 6.

2 Roughly chop all the vegetables and add them to a flameproof roasting pan. Pour over the olive oil and toss to coat. Roast in the hot oven until everything is caramelized and dark in colour.

3 Remove from the oven and put the pan on the hob/stovetop over medium heat. Add 1 litre/4 cups water and bring to a simmer scraping off all the nice sticky bits on the bottom of the pan. Continue to do this until the bottom of the roasting pan is clean.

4 Transfer the contents of the roasting pan to a pressure cooker or saucepan and add another 4 litres/16 cups water. In the pressure cooker, cook on full pressure for 1 hour. After 1 hour, allow to depressurize naturally. If using a pan on the hob/stovetop, bring up to a boil, then turn down to a simmer and let it tick over for 5 hours.

5 Pass through a fine chinois. Serve at once or allow to cool and keep in the fridge for up to 5 days.

Our go-to for nearly every veggie bowl. So versatile, great hot or cold, in winter or summer.

roasted shellfish soup

Serves 15

2kg mix of prawn, crab and/or lobster shells

1x spanish onion 2x carrots 1x garlic bulb

½x fennel bulb 2 sticks celery big drizzle olive oil

5g/2 tsp fennel seeds 10g/2½ tbsp coriander seeds 2x star anise

3g/1¼ tsp annatto seeds 200ml/scant 1 cup shoaxing wine 300ml/1¼ cups mirin

1 Preheat the oven to 180°C fan/200°C/400°F/Gas 6.

2 Add the shellfish shells to a roasting pan and roast in the hot oven until deep red and nice and caramelized. Meanwhile, roughly chop the onion, carrots, garlic, fennel and celery.

3 In a pressure cooker or pan, heat up the olive oil, add all the veg and fry until golden brown. Smash up the shells and add to the pan. Add the spices. Deglaze with the wine, then add the mirin. Scrape the bottom of the pan to release all the good bits. Cook to reduce the booze by half, then add 5 litres/20 cups water. Cook on full pressure for 1 hour. After 1 hour, allow to depressurize naturally. If using a pan on the hob/stovetop, bring up to a boil, then turn down to a simmer, skim off the scum and let it simmer for 5 hours.

4 Pass through a fine chinois. Serve at once or allow to cool and keep in the fridge for up to 5 days.

Just a bowl of this on its own with some good bread is bliss.

fish bone soup

Serves 15

3kg **fish bones (white fish)** 2x **onions** 1x **garlic bulb** 1x **fennel bulb** 2 sticks **celery** 10g/2½ tbsp **coriander seeds** 2x **star anise** 200ml/scant 1 cup **mirin**

1. Preheat the oven to 180°C fan/200°C/400°F/Gas 6.

2. Roughly chop the fish bones, onions, garlic, fennel and celery, and add them all to a flameproof roasting tray. Roast in the hot oven until everything is caramelized and sticky. Add the spices for the last 10 minutes of roasting.

3. Remove from the oven and put the pan on the hob/stovetop over medium heat. Add 1 litre/4 cups water and bring to a simmer scraping off all the nice sticky bits on the bottom of the pan. Continue to do this until the bottom of the roasting pan is clean.

4. Transfer the contents of the roasting pan to a pressure cooker or saucepan and add another 4 litres/16 cups water. In the pressure cooker, cook on full pressure for 1 hour. After 1 hour, allow to depressurize naturally. If using a pan on the hob/stovetop, bring up to a boil, then turn down to a simmer and let it simmer for 3 hours.

5. Pass through a fine chinois. Serve at once or allow to cool and keep in the fridge for up to 5 days.

Keep your fish bones and make this! Avoid oily fish bones, as they can make the soup bitter.

white chicken soup

3x **onions** 1x **garlic bulb** 2x **carrots**
½x **leek** 2kg **chicken wings**

1 Roughly chop the onions, garlic, carrots and leek. Add them to a pressure cooker with the chicken wings and 5 litres/20 cups water and cook on full pressure for 1 hour. Allow to depressurize naturally or, if you want an even creamier soup, let the steam out super quick and this will let the soup continually boil as it cools down, not allowing it to settle.

2 Alternatively, to cook on the hob/stovetop, add everything to a pan and bring to the boil. Turn down to a simmer and cook for 6–8 hours, skimming the scum off in the first hour. If you want a creamier soup, then boil for the first hour and the last half an hour (if you do this, you might have to top up with a little water, just keep an eye on levels).

3 Pass through a fine chinois. Serve at once or allow to cool and keep in the fridge for up to 5 days.

This is similar to the roast chicken wing soup (see opposite), but quicker to make and less hassle. It has a nice, white, creamy finish.

roast chicken wing soup

Serves 15

3x **onions** 1x **garlic bulb** 2x **carrots** ½x **leek**
2kg **chicken wings** drizzle **neutral oil**

1 Preheat the oven to 180°C fan/200°C/400°F/Gas 6.

2 Roughly chop the onions, garlic, carrots and leek, then add them to a flameproof roasting tray with the chicken wings and toss with the oil. Roast in the oven for 45–60 minutes until everything is caramelized.

3 Remove from the oven and put the tray on the hob/stovetop over medium heat. Pour in 1 litre/4 cups of the water. Bring it up to a simmer, scraping the bottom of the tray to get all the bits up that might have stuck. Do this until the bottom of the tray is clean.

4 Transfer the contents of the roasting tray to a pressure cooker or saucepan and add another 4 litres/16 cups water. In the pressure cooker, cook on full pressure for 1 hour. After 1 hour, allow to depressurize naturally. If using a pan on the hob/stovetop, bring up to a boil, then turn down to a simmer and let it tick over for 6 hours.

5 Pass through a fine chinois. Serve at once or allow to cool and keep in the fridge for up to 5 days.

The essence of chicken in a soup. Need I say more?

smoked ham soup

Serves 15

5x **spring onions** 2x **garlic bulbs** 300g **ginger** 2x **smoked ham hocks** 1x **pig's trotter**

1 Roughly chop the spring onions/scallions, garlic and ginger.

2 Add all the ingredients to a pressure cooker with 5 litres/20 cups water and cook on full pressure for 1 hour and 20 minutes. Allow to depressurize naturally. Alternatively, to cook on the hob/stovetop, add everything to a pan and bring to the boil. Turn down to a simmer and cook for about 5 hours.

3 Pass through a fine chinois (keep the meat from the hocks for another recipe, discard the veg). Serve at once or allow to cool and keep in the fridge for up to 5 days.

Lovely, smoky and gelatinous, I could neck this by the pint.

roasted beef and bone marrow soup

Serves 15

3x **onions** 2x **garlic bulbs** 3x **carrots** ½x **leek** 2 sticks **celery** 3kg **beef bones** 2kg **marrow bones**

1 Preheat the oven to 180°C fan/200°C/400°F/Gas 6.

2 Roughly chop the onions, garlic, carrots, leek and celery.

3 Add all the bones and vegetables to a flameproof roasting tray and roast in the hot oven until everything is caramelized and sticky.

4 Remove from the oven and put the tray on the hob/stovetop over medium heat. Pour in 1 litre/4 cups water. Bring it up to a simmer, scraping the bottom of the tray to get all the bits up that might have stuck. Do this until the bottom of the tray is clean.

5 Transfer the contents of the roasting tray to a pressure cooker or saucepan and add another 4 litres/16 cups water. In the pressure cooker, cook on full pressure for 1 hour. After 1 hour, allow to depressurize naturally. If using a pan on the hob/stovetop, bring up to a boil, then turn down to a simmer and let it tick over for 6–8 hours, skimming it every so often.

6 Pass through a fine chinois. Serve at once or allow to cool and keep in the fridge for up to 5 days.

Super beefy with a lovely mouthfeel.

how to make noodles

Serves 10

1kg/7 cups **strong white bread flour** 12.5g/12/3 tbsp **wheat gluten** 25ml/1½ tbsp **lye water** 12.5g/2½ tsp **fine salt**

1 In a mixing bowl add the flour and wheat gluten. Slowly start mixing together.

2 In a mixing jug/cup, measure out 375ml/1½ cups water and add the lye water and salt. Whisk together until the salt is completely dissolved.

3 Start adding the water solution to the flour. Once it's all added, leave it to mix for a good 5 minutes until it resembles a dough. Wrap it in clingfilm/plastic wrap and leave in the refrigerator overnight.

4 Take the dough out of the refrigerator a good hour before you want to start rolling it.

5 Set up a pasta machine and start by setting it on the widest setting. Cut the dough into 4 pieces and wrap 3 of them up in clingfilm so they don't dry out while you roll the first.

6 Roll the dough out so it is thin enough to go through the machine, then roll it through the machine a couple of times. Take the machine down to its next setting and roll through again. Repeat this a third time.

7 Now fold the dough back over itself and roll it through again. The layers should come together.

8 Keep going down the settings until you have a sheet about 3mm/⅛in thick.

9 To cut it into noodles, fit the spaghetti attachment. Cut the sheet to about 30cm/12in long, then roll it through the cutter, and that should be 1 portion of noodles done. Dust them in more flour and set aside.

10 Repeat with the remaining 3 portions of the dough.

These are some of the favourite toppings from the supper club days and what's served in the shops. Although specifically designed to go in certain bowls, have a little play around and mix it up a bit.

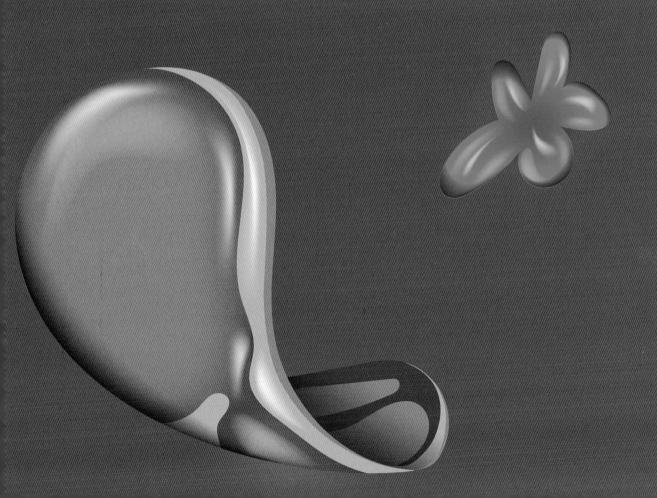

mapo tofu

Serves 4–6

50g **dried shiitake mushrooms** 1x **spanish onion**
30ml/2 tbsp **rapeseed oil** 50g/about 15x **garlic cloves** 100g **gochujang**
100g **tomato purée** 100ml/scant ½ cup **light soy sauce**
150ml/⅔ cup (see page 83) **house chilli oil** 350g **semi-firm tofu**
1 bunch, sliced **spring onions**

1. Soak the shiitakes in boiling water for at least 1 hour.

2. Finely chop the onion. Heat the oil in a medium pan and sweat off the onion and garlic for 8–10 minutes.

3. Drain the mushrooms (you can keep the stock to add to soups or other bits down the line). Either blitz the mushrooms in a food processor or finely chop by hand.

4. Add the mushrooms to the pan with the onion and garlic along with the gochujang and tomato purée/paste, and cook out slowly for 5 minutes. Then add the soy and chilli oil and cook out for another 5 minutes.

5. Turn off the heat. Chop the tofu into 1-cm/½-in cubes and add to the pan with the spring onions/scallions. Give it a good mix.

This is one we have on in the summer served cold as a mazesoba with a little garlic oil and tomato dashi. It is, however, just as nice served hot in a bowl.

fudgy eggs

Makes 1–6

500ml/ 2 cups **light soy sauce** 250g/ 1¼ cups **caster sugar**

300ml/ 1¼ cups **hot water** 1–6x **eggs**

1 Add the soy sauce, sugar and hot water to a saucepan and gently heat to dissolve the sugar. Set aside.

2 Have a bowl of iced water ready for egg dunking.

3 Bring a pan of water to a rolling boil. Lower the eggs gently into the water and boil for 6 minutes and 45 seconds. When the timer goes off, take them out and plunge them straight into the iced water. Leave for about 10 minutes.

4 Peel them in the iced water (it'll be easier to peel them under water). Once peeled, add them to the egg brine. Cover with white paper towels (don't use coloured as it'll stain the eggs) to help them to cure evenly. If you don't cover them, the eggs on the top of the brine will only be half cured.

5 Pop in the fridge overnight to cure. Overnight will be plenty of time to get them good and fudgy. You can leave them for longer, but the white will get harder – however it will still be good. I did an experiment at home and brined some for a month, they were intense to say the least.

I've tried to work out how many eggs I've peeled since I started Supa Ya and I reckon it's got to be over 32,000… that's a lot of eggs. I've tinkered with this recipe over the years and have simplified it to get the most consistent fudgy egg I could. You want a nice jammy yolk, almost toffee-like. Cooking times vary, depending on the size of the egg, so test one and then have another go. I'm going on UK medium/US large eggs (for larger eggs, add another 15 seconds or so, and for smaller eggs, reduce it by 15 seconds). This brine recipe is good to use a few times over, so don't bin it after one use; it'll keep in the fridge for a week.

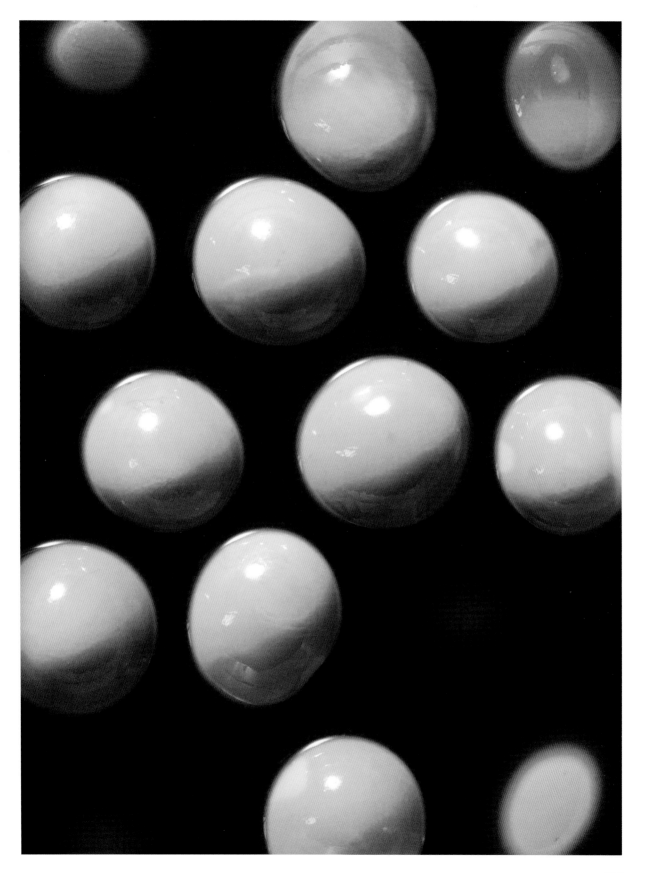

buttered chilli corn

Serves 5

50g/3½ tbsp **unsalted butter** (page 84) 50g **house chilli crisp**

250g/scant 2 cups **frozen corn, defrosted**

1. In a pan melt the butter and chilli crisp together. Add the corn and give it a good mix up.

2. It's ready to go.

Instead of the house chilli crisp, you can use Lao Gan Ma.

celeriac chashu

Serves 10

1x celeriac 60–75ml/4–5 tbsp **olive oil** pinch Maldon **sea salt**

500ml/2 cups **light soy sauce** 1 litre/4 cups **mirin** 250g/1¼ cups **caster sugar**

1x, roughly chopped **garlic bulb** 100g, roughly chopped **ginger**

1 Preheat the oven to 180°C fan/200°C/400°F/Gas 6.

2 Peel the celeriac/celery root and put it in a roasting pan. Dress it with the olive oil and a little Maldon salt. Roast in the oven until golden brown, a little charred around the edges and a knife goes through it easily.

3 Put the soy, mirin, caster/superfine sugar, garlic and ginger in a pan with 500ml/2 cups water and bring to the boil. Reduce to a simmer and cook for 45–60 minutes until reduced by half.

4 About halfway through the reduction, add the whole roasted celeriac to the glaze pan and continue to simmer, spooning the sauce over the celeriac every 5 minutes or so to give it a good glaze all over.

5 Once cooked, slice the celeriac into 2cm/¾in thick slices as a topping for your ramen bowl of choice. It can be used immediately, but for any left over, arrange the celeriac in a container, lining the slices up like a deck of cards, and pour the marinade over. Cover and refrigerate overnight for maximum flavour.

This was the first ever vegetarian bowl I did at the supper club about 5 months in. It proved so popular, I think I ended up running it for about 4 weeks.

115

braised octopus

Serves 10

1x **spanish onion** 5x **garlic cloves**
1x **small octopus** 600g **cherry tomatoes**
¼ bunch **oregano** ¼ bunch **dill** 500ml/2 cups **white wine**

1. Roughly chop the onion and smash the garlic cloves. Add them to a large pan with the rest of the ingredients and 1 litre/4 cups water. The pan needs to be deep enough so the octopus is fully submerged.

2. Bring up to the boil and then turn down to a simmer, and cover with a lid or some parchment paper. Simmer gently for a couple of hours until the octopus is nice and tender. Once cooked, turn off the heat and allow the octopus to cool down in its liquor. Leave it to rest overnight in the fridge.

3. The next day remove the octopus from its liquor and cut it into bite-size pieces. Strain the cooking liquor and reserve. This is now ready to use in the braised octopus, raw asparagus and fermented chilli bowl (see page 28).

A beautifully light, tender octopus. Light up the barbecue and give it a lick of smoke.

mortadella wontons and clams

Serves 6

1x **onion** 2x **garlic cloves** 150g **mortadella**
bunch **wild garlic** 45ml/ 3 tbsp **neutral oil** 300g **clams**
200ml/ scant 1 cup **white wine** 12x **wonton sheets** 1 beaten (optional) **egg**

1 Finely chop the onion, garlic, mortadella and wild garlic.

2 Heat the oil in a frying pan and gently sweat off the onion and garlic until soft. Leave to cool, then add the mortadella and a quarter of the wild garlic.

3 Place a deep pan – large enough to steam the clams – over medium heat. Once the pan is nice and hot, throw in the clams, the rest of the wild garlic and the white wine, then put a lid on and steam until the clams open; 4–5 minutes.

4 Let the clams cool down in the stock, then strain the clams, reserving the stock.

5 Remove about a third of the clams from their shells and finely dice them, then add this to the mortadella and onion mix. Give this a good stir.

6 Place a spoonful of the mix into the centre of 6 wonton sheets. Brush some water or egg wash round the edges of the sheets, then place another sheet on top. Press them closed really tightly, squeezing the air out. These are now ready to cook in the mortadella wontonmen, clams and wild garlic bowl (see page 34); the remaining clams are added to the bowl at the end.

This would be great just as a plate of food with a white wine sauce.

smoked bacon, morel and truffle mapo tofu

Serves 6

50g **dried morels** 5 slices **streaky bacon** 8x **garlic cloves** drizzle **neutral oil** 300ml/1¼ cups **guinness** 50g **tomato purée** 100g **gochujang** 100ml/scant ½ cup (page 83) **house chilli oil** 150ml/⅔ cup **light soy sauce** 350g **semi-firm tofu** 100g **black truffle** 5x **spring onions**

1. Soak the mushrooms in boiling water for at least 1 hour.

2. Chop the bacon and thinly slice the garlic. Heat the oil in a decent-sized frying pan over medium heat and add the bacon. As it starts to colour, add the garlic. Gently fry until the garlic starts to soften and colour.

3. Drain the mushrooms and keep the soaking liquid. Slice the mushrooms lengthways. Add to the pan and let them have a bit of time together, then deglaze the pan with the Guinness and cook to reduce it by three-quarters.

4. Add the tomato purée/paste and gochujang to the pan and cook for 5 minutes, then add the chilli oil to the pan along with the mushroom soaking liquid and soy, and cook to reduce by three-quarters.

5. Chop the tofu into 1-cm/½-in cubes. Finely chop the truffle and thinly slice the spring onions/scallions. Add the tofu to the pan, then turn off the heat and add the truffle and spring onions.

This is ridiculously over the top (in a good way). Pure decadence. I like to serve this with soft-boiled eggs, not the fudgy ones, so when you cut them open they add another layer of smut with their oozy yolks.

ham hock chashu

2x **garlic bulbs** 150g **ginger** 2x **smoked ham hocks** 5x **spring onions** (page 114) **celeriac chashu marinade**

1 Halve the garlic bulbs and roughly chop the ginger.

2 You will need a pan large enough to fit the hocks covered in plenty of water. Add the ham hocks, spring onions/scallions, garlic and ginger to the pan, bring to the boil, then turn down to a simmer. Pop a lid on and let it simmer for 3−4 hours until nice and tender. The meat should come away from the bone easily without having to persuade it.

3 Let it cool down in the stock (if you take it out of the stock to cool down, it will dry out and no one likes dry ropey meat). Once cooled, pick the meat from the bones, keeping it fairly chunky.

4 Marinate the ham hock meat in the celeriac chashu marinade, cover and place in the fridge overnight. You can strain the stock you cooked it in and use as a smoked ham soup for another ramen.

This is the ham we use on the Ham, Egg and Chips Mazesoba (see page 48). It's salty, sweet and chewy — it almost has a candied feel to it. Real moreish.

fried chicken

Serves 4

100g/ 3½ tbsp **fine salt** 4x (boneless for a bowl, bone-in for a plate of fried chicken) **chicken thighs**

250ml/ 1 cup **buttermilk** 50g **frank's hot sauce**

400g/ 4 cups **cornflour** 100g/ ¾ cup **plain flour** for frying **neutral oil**

1. Add the salt to 500ml/2 cups water and whisk to dissolve. This is your brine. Put the chicken thighs in the brine, cover and leave overnight in the refrigerator.

2. In a bowl, mix together the buttermilk and hot sauce. This is your wet dredge. In another bowl, mix together the cornflour/cornstarch and plain/all-purpose flour. This your dry dredge.

3. About an hour before you want to start frying, take the thighs out of the brine and put them in the wet dredge for 30 minutes.

4. Take the thighs out of the wet dredge and shake off any excess liquid. Place them in the dry dredge and really pack them in making sure they are completely covered. Leave them in the dry dredge for another 30 minutes.

5. Meanwhile, get a deep-fryer (or pan of oil if you're old school) up to 160°C/325°F.

6. Now to start frying. Take the thighs out of the dry dredge and shake off any excess flour. Lower them into the hot oil and cook until they reach an internal temp of 86°C/187°F (this sounds high, but fried chicken will take it and not dry out). When they hit 86°C/187°F, take them out of the fryer to drain and rest. You can sit them on a resting rack or just some paper towels.

7. Turn the fryer to 190°C/375°F. Fry the chicken again for 2–3 minutes until super crispy.

We do this every now and again as a stand-alone plate as it's so good. We normally serve it with an apricot glaze that I pilfered and changed a little from my mate Neil Rankin from our days at The John Salt. The chicken is so crunchy it stands up to sitting on top of a steaming bowl of noodles.

black bean sausage

Serves 4

5x **garlic cloves** 25g **preserved black beans** 10g/¼ cup **chopped chives** 250g **minced pork shoulder** 100g **minced pork fat** generous ½ tsp 3g/ **fine salt**

1 Finely chop the garlic and preserved black beans. Add them to a bowl with the chopped chives, minced/ground pork shoulder and fat, and the salt.

2 Lay some clingfilm/plastic wrap out on your work surface. Lay one-third of the mixture on top and roll it into a sausage shape, then wrap it tightly and tie the ends. Repeat this with the rest of the mixture, so you have 3 sausages in total.

3 Set a bamboo steamer over a pan of simmering water and gently steam the sausages in the clingfilm until cooked. Allow to cool, then transfer to the refrigerator to set.

4 When ready to serve, take the sausages out of the clingfilm and pan-fry them like you would normal sausages. Then get fancy and carve them into thick rounds before plating.

This was the star of the third-ever bowl at the supper club, but has never reared its ugly head at the shops yet... One day I'll drop it.

cumberland sausage tantanmen

Serves 10

1x **large onion** 8x **garlic cloves**

1kg **cumberland sausage** about 100ml/ scant ½ cup **neutral oil**

375ml/1½ cups (page 83) **house chilli oil** 125g **gochujang**

1 Finely chop the onion and garlic. Take the sausage meat out of the skins. Put enough oil into a fairly large saucepan so that it covers the bottom of the pan to a depth of about 5mm/¼in. Place it over medium heat – you want to get a good sizzle on the sausage.

2 Break up the sausage meat into about 1-cm/½-in chunks and add to the pan. Give it a good stir, breaking up the sausage meat and not letting it catch on the pan. Once the sausage meat is coloured nicely, add the onion and garlic. Carry on cooking for about 5 minutes to soften the onion. Add the chilli oil and the gochujang and turn down the heat to a simmer. Cook for about 20 minutes.

3 This is great served ramen-style, but equally as good served as a mazesoba or anywhere you'd use a ragù.

I first had dan dan noodles when I was working at Spitalfields market next door to Dumpling Shack, who kept me in dumplings and noodles all winter. I loved the hum of the dan dan sauce and, when I was in Tokyo, I came across tantanmen, which, like dan dan, is a dish of spicy minced/ ground pork or beef served over dry noodles or a soupy number. I wanted to do a version of it and a Cumberland sausage version just seemed a natural fit. We first served this up at Hackney Road and people lost their minds. We serve it in a spicy sesame miso soup. It's hot, tangy and numbing, but the flavour of the sausage still sings. After all, you still wanna know you're having bangers for tea.

pickles and ferments

We love pickling at Supa Ya and always have a pickle plate on the menu. We also use pickles a lot in the bowls – it's a great contrast to rich fatty soups and buttery toppings. Pickles help to cut through fattiness and keep your palate interested, making sure you want to go in for another spoonful. A lot of these recipes were cooked up by one of my best mates Lola, who helped us open the Dalston shop. She kept me sane for the first 6 months. Without her knowledge, sense of humour and tireless work ethic, I would have probably had about ten heart attacks.

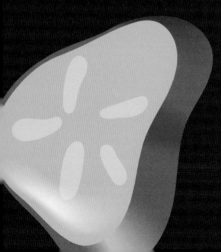

supa ya ramen pickles (pickled cucumbers)

Serves 15

2x **cucumbers** 200ml/scant 1 cup **rice wine vinegar**

100ml/scant ½ cup **light soy sauce**

1 If you're feeling frisky and don't mind the risk of losing a fingertip (we all have), then you can cut the cucumbers on a mandoline to about 3mm/⅛in thick. If not, a nice sharp knife will do. Slice them in rounds or, if you want to get fancy, you can do them on an angle.

2 In a bowl mix together the vinegar and soy. Add the cucumbers to the bowl, give them a good mix up and that's it. It really is that simple.

3 If you're using them the same day, you can leave them out at room temperature to quicken the pickle process. If not, whack them in the fridge and they'll be good whenever you need them.

This super-easy but super-effective pickle first made an appearance in the supper club days on a great little miso bowl with roast chicken, Iberico pork fat and a Tokyo-style togarashi. It's so easy to make — there's no brining or salting, just slice up the cucumbers, pour over the liquor and you're good to go. The pickles are ready in just half an hour, but they get better with age, so you can leave them in the back of your fridge and whip them out to stick in a sarnie when you get home late from the pub. This will serve about four people if using in bowls, with enough left over to have a little stash in the fridge for snacks.

smacked cucumbers

Serves 20

3x **cucumbers** 30g **ginger** 7x **garlic cloves**

300ml/ 1¼ cups **light soy sauce** 150ml/ ⅔ cup **rice wine vinegar**

100ml/ scant ½ cup **rice wine** 30ml/ 2 tbsp **sesame oil** 10g/ 2 tbsp **chilli flakes**

1. Either dice the cucumber into 1-cm/½-in cubes or slice lengthways, deseed and cut into semi-circles, whatever makes you feel good.

2. Finely chop the ginger and garlic.

3. Mix all the ingredients in a bowl and then leave it to sit out for a good few hours, mixing every now and again, so the cucumbers really take on the flavours.

4. Cover and store in the refrigerator for up to 1 month.

These are great with everything, we even use them in a smacked cucumber margarita.

bread and butter pickles

Serves 15

2x **cucumbers** 500ml/2 cups **white wine vinegar**

150g/¾ cup **caster sugar** 10g/1 tbsp **mustard seeds**

3g/½ tbsp **ground turmeric**

1. Cut the cucumbers into 1-cm/½-in cubes and place in a bowl.

2. Put the white wine vinegar, caster/superfine sugar, mustard seeds and ground turmeric into a pan with 150ml/⅔ cup water and bring to the boil.

3. Once boiling, pour over the cucumbers and leave to cool. Once cool, cover and refrigerate for up to 1 month.

These go on the cheeseburger mazesoba bowl (see page 66), but are equally good on their own or in a ham sandwich.

pickled daikon with gochujang

Serves 10

1x daikon 300ml/1¼ cups **white wine vinegar** 100g/¼ cup **caster sugar** 10g/2 tsp **fine salt** 15g/1 tbsp **gochujang** 3g/2 tsp **chilli flakes** pinch **red pepper powder**

1 Peel the daikon/mooli and cut it into 1-cm/½-in cubes and place in a bowl.

2 Put the white wine vinegar, caster/superfine sugar, salt, gochujang, chilli flakes and red pepper powder in a pan with 150ml/⅔ cup water and bring to the boil.

3 Once boiling, remove from the heat and pour over the daikon. Allow to cool, then cover and keep in the fridge for 1 month.

4 Sprinkle over with a light dusting of red pepper powder when serving.

Probably the first pickle we ever came up with and it's still on rotation. It tastes great, but be warned, when you open them after a few days they will smell awful...

pickled fennel

Serves 15

2x fennel 300ml/ 1¼ cups **white wine vinegar** 100g/ ½ cup **caster sugar** 15g/ 1 tbsp **fine salt** 2x **star anise** 10g/ 3½ tbsp **sichuan peppercorns** 10g/ 1½ tbsp **fennel seeds**

1 If you're feeling brave, thinly slice the fennel on a mandoline or slice as thinly as you can with a knife. Place the fennel in a bowl.

2 Put the white wine vinegar, caster/superfine sugar, salt, star anise, Sichuan peppercorns and fennel seeds in a pan with 100ml/scant ½ cup water and bring up to the boil.

3 Once boiling, pour over the fennel. Allow to cool, then cover and keep in the fridge for 1 month.

This is a lovely aromatic pickle, great on a pickle plate or with some canned fish or some stinky cheese.

pickled baby cucumbers

Makes 5

5x **baby cucumbers** 750ml/3 cups **white wine vinegar**
35g/3 tbsp **caster sugar** 5g/1 tsp Maldon **sea salt** 125g/8 tbsp **dijon mustard**
2g/1 tsp **caraway seeds** 10g/1 tbsp **mustard seeds**

1 If you want to speed up the pickling process, prick the cucumbers all over with a cocktail stick/toothpick. Put the cucumbers into a bowl and set aside.

2 Put the white wine vinegar, caster/superfine sugar, salt, mustard, caraway seeds and mustard seeds in a pan with 250ml/1 cup water and bring to the boil.

3 Once boiling, pour over the cucumbers. Allow to cool, then cover and leave to pickle at room temperature. If you haven't pricked the cucumbers, they will need 1 week to pickle; if they have been pricked, they will be ready in a couple of days. Store in the fridge for up to 1 month.

Great to leave whole to snack on while waiting for your drink.

pickled ginger

Serves 15

200g **ginger** 1x **garlic clove** 125ml/ ½ cup **white wine vinegar** 100g/ ¼ cup **caster sugar** 3g/ ½ tbsp **ground turmeric** 1x **star anise**

1 Peel the ginger and cut it into thin batons. Put into a bowl and set aside.

2 Smash the garlic and add it to a pan with the vinegar, sugar, turmeric, star anise and 50ml water. Bring to the boil. Once boiling, pour over the ginger and let cool. Cover and store in the fridge for up to 1 month.

This a fiery little number that helps lift up a super-rich fatty bowl. It's also great to eat when you have a cold.

pickled cauliflower

Serves 15

1x **cauliflower** 1 litre/ 4 cups **white wine vinegar** 250g/ 1¼ cups **caster sugar** 15g/ 1 tbsp **fine salt** 2g/ 4 tsp **saffron**

1 Break down the cauliflower into small florets and place in a bowl.

2 Put the white wine vinegar, caster/superfine sugar, salt and saffron in a pan and bring to the boil. Once boiling, pour over the cauliflower. Leave to cool, then cover and store in the fridge for up to 1 month.

This will make quite a lot, but what's the point in pickling anything less than a whole cauliflower?

pickled red chillies

Serves 15

250g **red chillies** 250ml/1 cup **white wine vinegar**

50g/¼ cup **caster sugar** 25g/2½ tbsp **wholegrain mustard**

generous ½ tsp 3g/ **fine salt** 2x **garlic cloves** 3 sprigs **fresh thyme**

1 Slice the chillies on the round as fat or thin as you like (I like them fairly chunky so you get a nice crunch). Place in a bowl and set aside.

2 Smash the garlic cloves and add to a pan with the vinegar, caster/superfine sugar, mustard, salt and thyme. Bring to the boil and then pour over the chillies. Ideally let them cool, then cover and let them sit overnight before eating. Store in the fridge for up to 1 month.

One of my favourites and great with slow-cooked fatty meats. We serve these with the braised shortrib and tofu whip (see page 144). It cuts through anything while giving a little tickle of heat. Not gonna lie, I have them on my Marmite toast at home.

pickled limes

Serves 10

5x limes — 125ml/½ cup **white wine vinegar** — 50g/¼ cup **caster sugar** — 5g/1 tbsp **pink peppercorns** — 3g/1 tbsp **fennel seeds**

1 Peel and segment the limes. Place the segments in a bowl.

2 Put the white wine vinegar, caster/superfine sugar, peppercorns and fennel seeds in a pan and bring to the boil.

3 Once boiling, pour over the limes. Leave to cool, then cover and store in the fridge for up to 1 month.

A great little citrus pickle that works well lifting green vegetables. It would probably be great turned into a granita.

house kimchi

Serves 15–20

1x **chinese cabbage** ½x **daikon** 3x **carrots**
5x **spring onions** 15g/1 tbsp **fine salt** 60g **ginger**
3x **garlic cloves** 30ml/2 tbsp **fish sauce** 300g **gochujang**
15g/4 tsp **caster sugar** 50ml/3½ tbsp **rice wine vinegar**
50g **momoya kimchi base**

1 Thinly slice the Chinese cabbage. Peel and grate the daikon/mooli and carrots. Thinly slice the spring onions/scallions.

2 Put the cabbage in a bowl, lightly salt with fine salt and set aside for 1 hour.

3 Peel the ginger and add it to a food processor with the garlic, fish sauce, gochujang, caster/superfine sugar, vinegar and kimchi base. Blitz to a paste.

4 Squeeze all the water out of the grated daikon and carrots. Wash and squeeze all the excess water out of the salted cabbage.

5 In a large bowl, combine the cabbage, daikon, carrots and paste and give it a good mix – get your hands in there and really massage the paste into all the veg. As we cheated and added kimchi base, you don't have to ferment this for weeks; it's good to eat straight away. Store at room temperature for up to 1 month.

We started making this to go in the Kimchi Double Double Bowl (see page 16), but it is just as good in its own right, and excellent in a cheese toastie.

fermented chillies

Makes 650g/5 cups

500g **red chillies** 150g **scotch bonnet chillies**
as needed **fine salt** as needed **caster sugar**

1 In a food processor add the chillies and blitz until you have a fairly fine mash.

2 Weigh the mash, then add 2% salt and 2% sugar. Give it a good mix, then transfer to an airtight container and let it ferment at room temperature for at least 2 days (ideally a week) out of direct sunlight. The longer you leave it, the funkier it will get. You might have to 'burp' it once in a while – this is when you open the jar slightly to release the build-up of gas.

3 Once you have got it to the level of funk you're happy with, transfer to the fridge and keep for up to 1 month.

We use this as a base for a lot of stuff. It can be added to soup to give it a kick, used to make hot honey (see page 90), or you can blitz it again with some vinegar to make a hot sauce. There's always some kicking about in the kitchen.

fermented tomatoes with seaweed

Makes 330g/2 cups

300g baby plum tomatoes
25g nori sheets 5g/1 tsp fine salt

1. In a sterilized Kilner/Mason jar, add the tomatoes, nori and salt. Cover with warm water. Close the lid and give them a good shake to dissolve the salt.

2. Leave for at least 1 week at room temperature to help the fermenting process.

3. It will be good to eat after a week.

These are really good blitzed and added to soups to give them a little funk.

snacks

This section is all about small plates to snack on or share. Equally as good to start a dinner with or to serve on their own whatever time of day!

tofu whip

Serves 4

340-g block firm tofu **50g miso** **30ml/ 2 tbsp olive oil**
1x garlic clove **juice of 1 lemon**

1 Add all the ingredients to a food processor and blitz for a good 5 minutes until you have a super-smooth glossy whip.

2 Put in an airtight container and keep it in the fridge for up to 5 days.

3 Serve up with your topping of choice and plenty of freshly toasted bread for dipping, such as naan spread with flavoured butter – my favourite is seaweed butter.

This is inspired by the hummus I made a lot of at Berber & Q, and later on with Bubala. I wanted something dippy you could mop up with a load of good bread. The tofu whip stays the same, but the toppings are endless. Here are a few favourites over the next few pages (see pages 142–147).

roast artichokes and green chilli glaze

Serves 4

500g **jerusalem artichokes** 45–60ml/3–4 tbsp **olive oil**
Maldon **sea salt** 100g **ginger** 25g **garlic** 450ml/scant 2 cups **maple syrup**
150ml/2/3 cup **light soy sauce** 1x **green chilli**

1 Preheat the oven to 160°C fan/180°C/350°F/Gas 4. Line a baking tray with parchment paper.

2 Scrub the Jerusalem artichokes and cut into 2.5-cm/1-in cubes. Toss them in the olive oil and sea salt, then arrange on the lined baking tray and roast in the oven until they're caramelized all over; this will take an hour or so.

3 Peel and roughly chop the ginger and smash the garlic, then put them both in a small pan with the maple syrup and soy. Cook over medium heat to reduce by half. It should be really glossy and sticky when done. Pass the glaze through a fine mesh sieve/strainer. Deseed and finely chop the chilli and add to the glaze.

4 When the artichokes are cooked, cover them with the glaze and they're good to go.

These are a textural delight: crispy, chewy and sticky. They are great on the tofu whip, but just as good as a little side with some green salad or as part of a rogue roast.

summer tomatoes and
green tomato dressing

Serves 6

500g green tomatoes 5x **jalapeños** 4x **garlic cloves**
1 bunch **coriander** 50ml/ 3½ tbsp **rapeseed oil** 10g/2 tsp Maldon **sea salt**
juice of 2 **limes** 200g **nice tomatoes**

1 Roughly chop the tomatoes and jalapeños, and smash the garlic. Add them to a food processor. Tear up the coriander/cilantro, stalks and all, and add to the food processor. Add the oil, salt and lime juice and blitz until you get the smoothest sauce possible. It should have the consistency of a proper salsa.

2 About 10 minutes before serving, cut your nice tomatoes. Dress the tomatoes liberally with the green tomato dressing. Let the dressing sink in for a while – they'll get on very well.

3 Spoon onto to a plate and more dressing over the top.

So good in the summer, but you can also do it with winter tomatoes, which we dabble in. Kinda Mexican in flavour, this dressing is almost a green salsa, zinging with jalapeño and lime juice. It goes so well with tomatoes, but you can just make a bowl of it and dip your tortilla chips in it.

glazed shortrib and pickled red chillies

Serves 6

3kg **beef shortribs** 1x **spanish onion** 100g **ginger**
100g **garlic cloves** 1 bunch **coriander** 500ml/2 cups **light soy sauce**
50ml/3½ tbsp **rice wine vinegar** 600ml/21/3 cups **shaoxing wine**
50g/¼ cup **caster sugar** 25g/about 4 **star anise** 100g/¾ cup **coriander seeds**
30g/4½ tbsp **fennel seeds** 100g/generous 1 cup **sichuan peppercorns**
2 litres/8 cups (pages 100–101) **chicken stock** about 30g (page 135) **pickled red chillies**

1. Cut the shortribs into individual ribs if it's a whole block. Roughly chop the onion and peel and roughly chop the ginger. Smash the garlic.

2. Add the shortribs, onion, ginger and garlic to a pan with the coriander/cilantro, soy, vinegar, caster/superfine sugar, star anise, coriander seeds, fennel seeds, Sichuan peppercorns and stock. Bring to a boil, then turn down to a simmer and cook until tender; about 3—4 hours. Alternatively, cook in a pressure cooker on full pressure for 1 hour 15 minutes and depressurize naturally.

3. Remove the meat from the pan and keep warm in a tray wrapped in clingfilm/plastic wrap so the meat doesn't dry out. Strain the cooking liquor and put it back into the pan, then reduce by about two-thirds so it becomes nice and glossy.

4. To serve on the tofu whip, shred the meat from the bones and warm the shredded meat up in a little of the sauce so it becomes nice and sticky. Serve with a load more sauce and pickled red chillies.

This is incredibly indulgent for a small plate, but would also be good as a centrepiece for a Sunday joint if you are inclined to have something a bit different — keep the ribs in one piece.

mushrooms, maple and soy

Serves 5

5x **garlic cloves** 50g **ginger** 100ml/ scant ½ cup **light soy sauce**

300g **ponzu** 100ml/ scant ½ cup **maple syrup** 150ml/ 2/3 cup **shaoxing wine**

10g/ 2½ tbsp **coriander seeds** 5g/ scant 1 tbsp **fennel seeds**

5g/ about 1 **star anise** 500g **mixed mushrooms**

1. Smash the garlic and peel and roughly chop the ginger. Add them to a pan with all the other ingredients apart from the mushrooms. Bring to the boil, then turn down the heat to low and simmer for 30 minutes.

2. Turn the heat off and allow to infuse for 1 hour.

3. Strain and return the strained liquid to the pan. Roughly chop the mushrooms and add to the liquor. Bring back to the boil, then turn off the heat.

4. Can be served warm or cold. Always keep the mushrooms in the liquor (they're better the next day after they've had a night in their bath).

For a mushroom starter, this is super light. Lightly poached mushrooms — so they don't go spongy — are a glorious thing. If you keep them in the marinade for a day or two, they get better and better. This marinade would also be great for poaching fish or chicken or as a nice seasoning to cut through a soup.

caramelized hispi cabbage and smoked chicken butter

Serves 2

1x **hispi cabbage**   as needed **chicken stock**

smoked chicken butter

1/4x **smoked chicken**   500g/ 4½ sticks **lightly salted butter**

1 Start by making the smoked chicken butter. Shred the meat off the bird and set aside. Melt the butter in a pan and add the chicken bones. Bring to a simmer and allow to tick over for 30 minutes. Turn off the heat and allow the bones to infuse for a good few hours. Strain the butter and put it in the fridge.

2 Slice the hispi from tip all the way to the bottom. Lightly oil a frying pan and get it nice and hot. Place the cabbage in the pan cut-side down. Turn the heat down and cook it fairly slowly so it colours nicely. Add a few knobs/pats of the butter to the pan to help it on its way.

3 Add a ladle of chicken stock and let this emulsify with the butter, then start to spoon over the cabbage so the other side starts cooking. You might have to add more stock and butter as the cabbage will suck it up. Keep the cabbage cut-side down and cook until a knife slips in nicely.

4 Flip the cabbage for the last 5 minutes of cooking and spoon the remaining sauce over the cut side. By now the cabbage will be coloured nicely and be full of sauce. Add some of the reserved shredded smoked chicken to the sauce.

5 Serve the cabbage cut-side up with some of the smoky buttery sauce poured all over.

I love cabbage. It's so versatile. And the way this is cooked down with stock and butter, so it soaks up all those juices like a sponge, is one of life's greatest pleasures. (God I need to get out more.)

kohlrabi and cabbage salad, hot mustard ranch and nori

Serves 4

1x **kohlrabi** ½x **white cabbage** 4x **nori sheets**

hot mustard ranch

250g **mayonnaise** 125g **sour cream** 125g **crème fraîche** 25g/5 tsp **hot sauce** 100g/3 tbsp **english mustard** 1x **garlic clove** ½ bunch **dill** ½ bunch **chives**

1. For the hot mustard ranch, in a bowl combine the mayonnaise, sour cream, crème fraîche, hot sauce and mustard. Finely grate the garlic into it. Chop the herbs (don't worry about picking the dill, no one's got time for picking herbs... pointless) and add them too. Mix everything together and set aside.

2. Peel and dice the kohlrabi into 1-cm/½-in dice (you can keep this in water until needed). Very finely shred the cabbage, kebab-shop style.

3. Put the veg in a mixing bowl, add a couple of good dollops of the ranch and mix well – it should be really saucy.

4. In a Nutribullet (or something similar) blitz the nori sheets to a powder.

5. Place the salad in a serving bowl and, if you want to get cheffy (this is about as cheffy as it gets with us), put the nori powder in a tea strainer and sift it all over, otherwise just get your fingers in there and give it a good pinch all over.

Ranch dressing just bangs. Pimped up here with the heat of English mustard and the tang of hot sauce, it was described by one critic as a 'face slap of a salad'. Nuff said.

151

chilli fried peas with green pil pil and goat's curd

Serves 1

100g **frozen peas** (drizzle (page 83)) **house chilli oil**

green pil pil

30g/ about 10 **garlic cloves** 250ml/ 1 cup **olive oil**

5g/ 1 tsp **fine salt** 25g/ 2 heaped tbsp **korean red pepper powder**

½ bunch **parsley** 1 bunch **basil** 6–7 chunks **goat's curd**

1. For the green pil pil, finely slice the garlic, then, in a frying pan, heat the olive oil, garlic, salt and red pepper powder and very gently fry the garlic until golden. Allow to cool.

2. Transfer to a food processor and add the herbs. Blitz to a smooth paste.

3. Quickly blanch the peas in boiling water to defrost them, then refresh them in cold water and drain.

4. In a frying pan, heat the house chilli oil. Add the peas and gently fry for a few minutes, then remove from the heat and mix in at least 2 tablespoons of the green pil pil.

5. Serve the dressed peas while still warm, topped with small chunks of goat's curd. The curd will melt slightly into the peas and help cut through the spice.

This is super fragrant, slightly numbing, floral. Let the cheese sink in a little so it starts melting and releases that tang, which will cut through the heat.

twice-baked potato, miso butter and parmesan

Makes 1

1x **baking potato**   for grating **parmesan**

miso butter

250g **good miso**   250g/2¼ sticks softened **unsalted butter**

1. In a food processor blend the miso and butter together until completely smooth and emulsified. Cover and keep this in the fridge for up to 2 weeks or freeze in single portions to defrost at room temperature and use when needed.

2. Preheat the oven to 200°C fan/220°C/425°F/Gas 7.

3. Rub a little bit of the miso butter over the potato and place on a baking sheet. Put on the top shelf of the oven and cook for about 30 minutes.

4. Take out from the oven and carefully rub more butter over the potatoes. Turn the oven down to 160°C fan/180°C/350°F/Gas 4 and cook for another 45 minutes.

5. Take the potatoes out of the oven and cut them in half. Scoop the insides of the potatoes into a bowl, add 1 tablespoon of miso butter to the flesh of each potato and mix it in. Put the potato flesh back in the skins.

6. Grate a ton of Parmesan over the potatoes and place under a hot grill/broiler until the cheese is golden brown.

A daft take on a national treasure with amped up umami levels going through the roof. So cheesy, so good. S'pose you could serve it with a side salad.

crispy potatoes and smacked cucumbers
with hot honey and sesame dressing

Serves 4

4x large **maris piper potatoes**

salt for deep-frying **neutral oil** Maldon **sea salt**

to serve

drizzle, warmed (page 90) **hot honey** (page 126) **smacked cucumbers**

drizzle (page 86, omitting the chilli paste) **spicy sesame dressing**

handful chopped **green onions** pinch **togarashi**

1. Peel and chop the potatoes as you would do for roasties, then parboil them in salted water until nice and soft. Drain in a colander and let them steam dry.

2. When the potatoes are cool, toss them in the colander to rough them up a bit — this will create plenty of edges to get crispy in the deep-fryer.

3. Either in a pan or a deep-fryer, heat the oil to 180°C/350°F, or until a cube of bread browns in 30 seconds.

4. Add the potatoes to the hot oil and fry until golden brown and super crispy.

5. Once cooked, remove to a bowl and hit them with a load of Maldon sea salt — it's important to do this while still hot, so the salt sticks to the spuds.

6. Arrange the potatoes on a plate, drizzle with the hot honey, spoon a load of the cucumbers over the top and then drizzle with the sesame dressing. Finish with some chopped green onions and a pinch of togarashi.

If you have the honey, cucumbers and sesame dressing all ready to go, then this is a dish you can just throw together with minimal effort. It's a banger.

miso and ogleshield grilled cheese, egg yolk and soy dipping sauce

Serves 1

100g **ogleshield cheese** 25g **mozzarella cheese** 10g/2 tsp **miso** 2 slices **white bread** 30g/2 tbsp, plus extra for spreading **butter** 2 slices **american cheese** 30ml/2 tbsp **neutral oil**

dipping sauce

50ml/3½ tbsp (page 83) **house soy** 1x **egg yolk**

1. To make the dipping sauce, all you need to do is put the house soy in a small bowl or shallow dish, then drop the egg yolk into it, keeping it intact. Too easy.

2. Finely chop the cheeses, then mix them together in a small bowl with the miso.

3. Butter both sides of both slices of bread. Take one slice of bread and top with one slice of American cheese. Spread the cheesy mix evenly over the top, then put the other American slice on top of that and squeeze it down a little. Finish with the second slice of bread on top of that.

4. Get a frying pan over medium–low heat on the hob/stovetop. The key to this is cooking it slowly so the cheese starts to melt before the bread gets too crispy. Add the oil to the pan then add the 30g/2 tablespoons butter and get it foaming. Carefully lower the sandwich into the pan. Fry gently on both sides until the cheese is starting to ooze and the bread is a lovely golden-brown colour and crunchy; it'll probably be good after 3–4 minutes on both sides, and if the pan is starting to look a little dry, don't be scared of adding a load more butter.

Everyone loves grilled cheese sandwiches. This one's a little richer with the addition of the miso. It's great served up with some pickled baby cucumbers. Use cheap white sliced bread for this – sourdough is too cumbersome.

french onion dip and crispy chicken skin

Serves 4

300g **chicken skin** Maldon **sea salt** 2x **spanish onions** 3x **garlic cloves** 30ml/2 tbsp **neutral oil** knob/pat **unsalted butter** 1x **star anise** 2g/1 tsp ground **sichuan peppercorns** 10g/3½ tsp **plain flour** 200ml/scant 1 cup **rice wine** 800ml/scant 3½ cups (page 101) **roast chicken wing soup** 50g **sour cream** 50g **kewpie mayo** good sprinkle **togarashi** good sprinkle **chopped chives**

1 Preheat the oven to 170°C fan/190°C/375°F/Gas 5.

2 Lay the chicken skin on a chopping board. With a sharp knife, try and scrape off the majority of the fat from under the skin (this will help the skin crisp up in the oven). Place a wire rack inside a baking tray and arrange the chicken skin (with the outer skin side up) on the rack (you will need to work in batches). Sprinkle over some Maldon sea salt. Roast in the oven for about 15 minutes until golden brown and crispy — keep an eye on it. You'll have to do this in batches, so set aside a good hour or so to get these done before you're ready to eat, or you can do them the day before and keep them in an airtight container layered between some paper towels so they don't go soft.

3 Now get the French onion soup part of the dish on the go, as it'll have to chill before you add the dip element to it. Thinly slice the onions and garlic.

4 In a deep sauté pan, heat the oil and butter until the butter is foaming. Add the onions and sweat them down over fairly low heat until soft and beginning to colour. Add the spices and garlic, and continue to cook until the onions take on a deep golden-brown colour.

5 Stir in the plain/all-purpose flour, then deglaze the pan with the rice wine. Cook to reduce until it has evaporated.

6 Now add the chicken soup and reduce right down until it's almost completely disappeared and you have mainly sticky onions left. Transfer to a bowl and set aside to cool completely – even better if you can get it in the fridge overnight.

7 When you are ready to serve, take the onions out of the fridge and mix in the sour cream and Kewpie mayo. Sprinkle with a healthy dose of togarashi and chopped chives and serve with the chicken-skin dippers.

This is a fun little mash-up of the American French onion dip (made with sour cream and mayo) and French onion soup (with all those deeply caramelized onions). Instead of serving it with crisps à la America or croutons à la France, we're going to use crispy chicken skin.

black radish noodles with green peppercorn crab and xo butter

Serves 1

70g **black radish or turnip** 30g **crab**

green peppercorn sauce

100g **ginger** 100g/approx. 15 **garlic cloves** 100g/4½ tbsp **green peppercorns in brine** 100ml/scant 1/2 cup **oyster sauce** 40ml/2½ tbsp **light soy sauce** 5x **vine tomatoes** 1 bunch **coriander** grated zest and juice of 2 **limes** (page 75) **xo butter**

1 For the green peppercorn sauce, peel and slice the ginger and smash the garlic. Put them in a food processor with the peppercorns, oyster sauce and soy sauce, and blitz together until smooth. Transfer to a mixing bowl. Peel, deseed and finely chop the tomatoes and finely chop the coriander/cilantro, then add them to the bowl along with the lime zest and juice. Mix well.

2 Peel the black radish or turnip, then work it through a Japanese mandoline or a spiralizer. You can keep these in water until needed.

3 Add the veg noodles to a mixing bowl and add 40g of the green peppercorn dressing. Mix the noodles into the dressing so they are all coated.

4 Place the coated noodles into serving bowls and dress with how much crab your bank balance allows. Warm some of the XO butter in a pan and spoon over.

A perfect little summery noodle salad minus the carbs. The only dilemma is how decadent you want to be with the crab... I'll leave that with you.

crab fried rice with garlic butter and tobacco onions

Serves 1

150g **cooked cold rice** for frying **neutral oil**

25g **brown crab meat** 50g **white crab meat**

garlic butter

250g/2¼ sticks, softened **unsalted butter**

3x **garlic cloves** 1/3 bunch **coriander** 1/3 bunch **parsley**

1/3 bunch **chives** pinch **ground sichuan peppercorns**

tobacco onions

50g/ 3 tbsp **hot sauce** 500ml/ 2 cups **buttermilk** 200g/ 1½ cups **plain flour**

50g/ ¼ cup **light brown sugar**

20g/ 2 tbsp **korean red pepper powder**

20g/ 3 tbsp **ground cumin** 20g 5 tbsp **ground coriander**

20g/ scant 2 tbsp **ground mustard seeds**

2x **spanish onions** for deep-frying **vegetable oil**

1. For the garlic butter, grate the garlic into the butter. Finely chop the coriander/cilantro, parsley and chives and add to the butter along with the ground peppercorns. Give it a good mix up, cover and keep in the fridge until needed.

2. For the tobacco onions, in a bowl mix the hot sauce with the buttermilk. In a separate bowl mix the plain/all-purpose flour, sugar and ground spices.

3. Thinly slice the onions and put them in the buttermilk mixture. Leave to marinate for an hour or so.

4. Either in a pan or a deep-fryer, heat the oil to 180°C/350°F, or until a cube of bread browns in 30 seconds.

5. Take the onions out of the buttermilk and shake the excess off. Dredge in the spiced flour and give them a shake. Deep-fry until golden brown.

6. Drain on paper towels and hit them with a load of salt as soon as they're out of the oil. Keep on the paper towels until ready to use.

7. Get a frying pan nice and hot and add some oil. Add the rice and start frying. Don't overcrowd the pan as it'll end up steaming and not frying. Once the rice is nicely fried, add 2 tablespoons of the garlic butter and give it a mix. Take off the heat and dollop in some of the brown crab meat so it starts to melt in. Finish with loads of white crab meat and top with the tobacco onions.

So good when the crab melts into the butter and you end up with this garlicy crabby rice, super indulgent. Try using day-old rice to fry — never use freshly cooked rice, you'll have a stinker.

duck fat hash browns with english ham, kewpie mayo and caviar

Serves 4

1kg **duck fat** 3x **garlic cloves** few sprigs **thyme**
500g **maris piper potatoes** for deep-frying **neutral oil**
to serve **kewpie mayo** sliced, to serve **english ham** to serve **caviar**

1. Gently heat the duck fat in a pan and add the garlic and thyme. Very gently simmer for 30 minutes to infuse the fat. Remove the garlic and thyme.

2. Peel the potatoes and use a spiralizer to spiralize them into potato noodles. You can grate the potatoes if you don't have a spiralizer. Squeeze all the water out.

3. Add the potatoes to the duck fat and cook out really slowly over low heat until they're soft, not crunchy, you want the kind of consistency where you're able to easily put your finger through them. Once the potatoes are nice and soft, drain through a fine mesh sieve/strainer, squeezing the duck fat out.

4. Line a Tupperware box with some clingfilm/plastic wrap (you want one small enough so when the potato is spread out in it, it'll be about 2.5cm/1in high and compact to the sides) and spread the potato out in it. Cover with clingfilm and place a slightly smaller Tupperware box on top and weigh it down with a can of beans or something weighty. Leave to set in the fridge overnight.

5. The next day, take your slab of hash brown out of the fridge and turn it out onto a chopping board. Trim the edges and cut it into hash brown-sized rectangles.

6. Either in a pan or a deep-fryer, heat the oil to 180°C/350°F, or until a cube of bread browns in 30 seconds. Deep-fry the hash browns until golden and crispy.

7. To serve, squeeze on some Kewpie mayo, layer up some English ham and spoon on some caviar. Better than a McDonald's hash brown any day. Well, nearly.

You need quite a lot of duck fat for this recipe, but you can use it again and again, so it won't be a wasted purchase.

fennel, garlic and hot pepper sausage with braised mussels, clamato juice and prickly oil

Serves 1

10g/1½ tbsp **fennel seeds** 100g **garlic cloves** 1kg **minced pork** 250g **minced pork fat** 100g/2/3 cup **red pepper powder** 30g/¼ cup **cracked black pepper** 25g/5 tsp **fine salt**

prickly oil

500ml/2 cups **rapeseed oil** 100g/2¼ cups **sichuan peppercorns**

braised mussels

250g **mussels** 125ml/½ cup **white wine** 215ml/scant 1 cup **clamato juice**

1. For the fennel, garlic and hot pepper sausage, toast the fennel seeds in a dry frying pan and grind to a powder using a mortar and pestle or spice grinder. Transfer to a bowl. Mince the garlic and add to the bowl along with the minced/ground pork and fat, spices and salt. Mix everything together really well. If you have a nice butcher, you could ask him to put the mixture in sausage skins for you, if not, just roll them into golf ball-sized balls.

2. For the prickly oil, put the oil and Sichuan peppercorns in a pan and slowly bring it up to 110°C/225°F. Remove from the heat, infuse overnight, then strain.

3. If you're lucky enough to have had the sausages made for you, then roast these in the oven or pan-fry them until cooked through. If you have made them into meatballs, then pan-fry them all over until nice and crispy.

4. For the braised mussels, clean the mussels, removing the beards and any grit. Put a pan with a lid over the heat and get it nice and hot. Throw the mussels in, add the wine and put the lid on so they start steaming.

5. Cut the sausage, if using, into 2.5-cm/1-in chunks – you want 2 sausages per person or 7–8 meatballs per person. When the mussels start to open, throw in the sausages and a glass of clamato juice. Give it a good mix up.

6. Serve in bowls with a load of the prickly oil drizzled over the top.

Perfect as a bowl on its own eaten like moules marinière, or bung some noodles in and have it as a ramen. Don't skimp on the prickly oil, you wanna feel like you've just walked out of the dentist after eating it.

salt beef hash with pickled greens and egg yolk sauce

Serves 1

2x **maris piper potatoes** Maldon **sea salt**
15ml/1 tbsp, plus extra for deep-frying **neutral oil** 1x **onion** 2x **garlic cloves**
100g **salt beef** 50g **pickled greens**

egg yolk sauce

4x **egg yolks** 15ml/1 tbsp (page 83) **house soy**
15ml/1 tbsp **rice wine** 2g/a pinch **ground sichuan pepper**
225ml/scant 1 cup **rapeseed oil**

1. For the egg yolk sauce, blitz the egg yolks, soy sauce, rice wine and pepper in a food processor until fully combined. As you would make a mayo, slowly drizzle in the oil while blending until you have a lovely smooth emulsion.

2. Peel the potatoes and cut into 2.5-cm/1-in chunks. Parboil the potatoes in salted water until soft. Drain and fluff up in a colander.

3. In a pan or a deep-fryer, heat the neutral oil to 180°C/350°F, or until a cube of bread browns in 30 seconds. Deep-fry the potato cubes until super crispy and golden brown. Drain, season and set aside.

4. Chop the onion, thinly slice the garlic and cut the beef into 2-cm/¾-in pieces. Place a frying pan over medium heat and add 15ml/1 tablespoon oil. Add the onion, then once it starts to soften and colour a little, add the salt beef. Cook until the salt beef gets some colour on it and softens. Then, add the garlic and keep everything going for a few minutes. Throw in the potatoes at the end as you want these to stay crispy. Finish by mixing in the pickled greens. To serve, spoon the salt beef hash onto a plate and generously drizzle over the sauce.

You can find pickled mustard greens in Asian supermarkets.

raw beef with fermented chillies, kashk and fresh apple

Serves 3

360g per person **beef fillet** 1x **apple (pink lady)** 15ml/1 tbsp **sesame oil**

small pinch **salt** 18g/3 tsp (page 138) **fermented chillies** generous grating **kashk**

1 Dice the beef fillet into 5-mm/¼-in pieces. Dice the apple into a similar size.

2 Dress the beef with a little sesame oil and salt, then spoon a little of the fermented chillies over the beef. Grate loads of the kashk over. Dress with a good spoonful of the diced apple and finish with a little drizzle of the house chilli oil.

Kashk is a fermented whey product made from hanging yogurt then letting it dry out. Some are soft, but I like the hard ones you can grate. It has a cheesy, tangy flavour, which works great with the apple.

desserts

We only have a few desserts on at any one time – apart from the iconic noodle ice cream, which is always on – so we always try and have something chocolatey on and something creamy.

noodle ice cream with miso caramel

Serves 4

1.2 litres/5 cups **whole milk** 1.1 litres/4½ cups **double cream**

500g **noodle scraps or bought ramen noodles**

250g/1¼ cups **caster sugar** 12x **egg yolks**

miso caramel

400g/2 cups **caster sugar** 250ml/1 cup **double cream** 50g **miso**

1 In a deep pan, add the milk, double/heavy cream and noodles. Very slowly bring to a simmer, stirring often so the noodles don't catch and you don't scorch the milk and cream. Once up to a simmer, take it off the heat and place a lid on it or cover the top with clingfilm/plastic wrap so it is sealed. Infuse for 1 hour.

2 Meanwhile, in a large bowl, whisk the caster/superfine sugar and egg yolks together until smooth and creamy.

3 Once infused, strain the milk and cream mixture through a fine sieve/strainer, making sure to squeeze all the goodness out of the noodles, as that'll be where most of the flavour is. You want to get every last drop.

4 Add half the milk mixture to the egg yolks and whisk until completely combined. Add the rest of the milk mixture and whisk again.

5 Pour it into a clean pan and place over a very low heat. Cook it out really slowly, stirring in a figure of eight so you get into the sides of the pan. Cook the custard until it coats the back of a spoon or, if you want to get technical, until it reaches 83°C/181°F.

6 Pass it again through a fine sieve just in case there's a few lumps and transfer it to a container. Leave it to cool. When it's cool enough, cover with the lid and pop it in the fridge overnight to chill properly.

7 The next day, working in batches, churn the custard in an ice-cream machine, then freeze overnight.

8 To make the miso caramel, put the sugar and 150ml/⅔ cup water in a pan and heat gently until it forms a light caramel. Don't whisk it, you don't want it to crystallize. Once it's at caramel stage, take it off the heat and whisk in the cream. Finally whisk in the miso.

9 Serve the ice cream with some miso caramel drizzled over the top.

I'm not one for making desserts really. Coming up through kitchens, you always did a bit of pastry, but it's always the last thing on my mind when I'm writing a menu. I knew I wanted something unique to Supa Ya when we opened in Dalston, but what on earth could it be? I'd been making a lot of noodles at home, messing about making different bowls and testing stuff out. Whenever I made noodles, there was always loads of trim going in the bin, and this killed me – I hate waste in kitchens, so what could I do with it? Then, one day, the old lightbulb moment happened: noodle ice cream. Could work, I thought. You can infuse milk and cream with basically anything and make ice cream. Momofuku were trailblazing years ago with their cereal milk, and people were making brown bread ice cream and croissant ice cream, in fact the first pub I worked at – nearly 20 years ago – we were serving Christmas pudding ice cream during winter. So why not noodle ice cream?

I bought an ice-cream machine and went to work. The first few trials went pretty well. Toby tried it and loved it. It's been on the menu since day one and will never not be – it's still our best-selling dessert and a real point of conversation with newbies to the shop. This is one recipe that I had to tinker with a lot to get right, but here it is in all its glory.

salted caramel and sichuan truffles

Makes 20

100g/2¼ cups **sichuan peppercorns** 400g/4 cups **cocoa powder**

400g/2 cups **caster sugar** 400ml/scant 1¾ cups **double cream**

30g/2½ tbsp **soft brown sugar** 55g/3½ tbsp **unsalted butter**

20g/5 tsp Maldon **sea salt** 400g **dark chocolate**

1. Blitz the peppercorns to a fine powder in a food processor or blender. Transfer to a bowl, add the cocoa powder and mix really well.

2. Put the caster/superfine sugar in a pan over low heat and cook gently until it becomes a caramel. Add the double/heavy cream and whisk until fully mixed in. Add the brown sugar, butter, salt and dark/bittersweet chocolate. Stir to melt everything together.

3. Line a shallow dish with a few layers of clingfilm/plastic wrap and pour the mix in. Set overnight in the fridge.

4. The next day cut into squares and dust them in the cocoa powder mix to coat.

A decadent little chocolate that leaves you with a lovely numbing feeling when you don't expect it.

tofu and coconut pudding, miso cookie crumble

Serves 2–3

350g **semi-firm tofu** 85g **kaya (coconut jam)**

miso cookie crumble

150g **agave syrup** 150g/1¼ sticks **unsalted butter** 75g/6 tbsp **soft brown sugar** 100g/scant 1 cup **tahini** 1x **egg** 1x **egg yolk** 250g/scant 2 cups **plain flour** 2g/½ tsp **bicarbonate of soda** 15g/2½ tbsp **black and white sesame seeds** Maldon **sea salt**

1. For the pudding, in a food processor blitz together the tofu and kaya until smooth (the same as the tofu whip). It's that easy. Set aside.

2. In a pan, bring the agave syrup to a boil and cook until lightly caramelized. Take it off the heat and whisk in the butter. Transfer to a bowl and let cool. Once cooled, add the sugar, tahini, egg and egg yolk. Mix together.

3. In another bowl, sift the flour and bicarbonate of soda together. Add the wet mixture to the dry mixture and mix until it forms a dough. Roll into a cylinder and wrap in clingfilm. Place in the freezer for 2–3 hours or ideally overnight.

4. Preheat the oven to 160°C fan/180°C/350°F/Gas 4. Line a baking sheet. Unwrap the log and slice it into 1-cm/½-in rounds. Arrange on the baking sheet and sprinkle with sesame seeds and little Maldon salt. Bake for 12 minutes, turning the baking sheet after 6 minutes for an even cook. To serve, spoon some of the tofu pudding into bowls and either crumble some of the cookies over the top or serve the cookies on the side to use as dunkers.

When served chilled, this sweet whipped tofu takes on an almost custardy quality that is just so satisfying.

chocolate mousse with lemon and lime melon

Serves 6

300g **dark chocolate** 12x **egg whites**

6x **egg yolks** 40g/ 3¼ tbsp **caster sugar**

marinated melon

1x **galia melon** grated zest and juice of **1 lemon** grated zest and juice of **1 lime**

20g/ 5 tsp **caster sugar** 1g/ pinch **togarashi**

1 First make the marinated melon. Cut the melon into 1-cm/½-in cubes. Mix the melon with the citrus zest and juice, caster/superfine sugar and togarashi and leave to marinate for 1 hour.

2 Melt the dark/bittersweet chocolate in a heatproof bowl set over simmering water, making sure the bottom of the bowl doesn't touch the water.

3 In another bowl, whisk the egg whites to soft peaks. Add the caster/superfine sugar to the egg whites and whisk again to stiff peaks.

4 In a third bowl, whisk the egg yolks, then add the beaten yolks to the melted chocolate and mix well so that it comes together.

5 Add a quarter of the egg whites to the chocolate and mix in very quickly until completely combined. Very carefully fold in the remaining egg whites.

6 Serve the chocolate mousse in bowls with the melon spooned over.

This is a super-simple chocolate mousse, served with spicy, citrusy melon.

yuzu pannacotta and sesame seed brittle

Serves 4

2.5x **gelatine sheets** 300ml/ 1¼ cups **whole milk**
400ml/ scant 1¾ cups **double cream** 50g/ ¼ cup **caster sugar** 1x **yuzu**

sesame seed brittle

120g/9 tbsp unsalted **butter** 200g/ 1 cup **caster sugar** 15g/ 2½ tbsp **white sesame seeds** 15g/ 2½ tbsp **black sesame seeds**

1. Soak the gelatine sheets in cold water for a couple of minutes until soft.

2. Add the milk, double/heavy cream and caster/superfine sugar to a pan and heat to just below boiling. Peel the yuzu. Turn off the heat and add the yuzu skin.

3. Squeeze out the excess water from the gelatine and add it to the pan. Give it a good mix so it all melts. Cover and leave to infuse for at least 2 hours.

4. Strain into a jug/pitcher and then pour into ramekin-size moulds. Cover and leave to set in the fridge for at least a few hours or overnight if you can.

5. For the brittle, line a baking tray with baking parchment.

6. In a saucepan combine the butter, sugar and 50ml water over medium heat. As it starts to colour, add the sesame seeds. Cook out to a fairly dark caramel and then pour out onto the baking tray. Allow to cool, then break into shards.

7. Serve the pannacotta with shards of brittle.

A really nice light summer pudding.

You might already have a lot of this stuff if you're a keen cook, but here are a few little things we like to use in the kitchen to make our lives easier...

·   A decent-sized stockpot — you want something that holds at least 10 litres — sounds big but making soup in a pan not big enough is a nightmare.

·   Pressure cooker — if you are going down that route.

·   A few different-sized saucepans and frying pans.

·   Whisks — get a fairly small one... you don't want to be trying to whisk a bowl of soup with a massive balloon whisk.

·   A good set of tongs.

·   Noodle baskets — try and find a solid metal one with a wooden handle, the plastic ones are too flimsy and tend to fall apart quicker.

·   A spider — good for lifting eggs out of the pan, also good if you can't find any noodle baskets. I used a spider for my noodles for about 3 months at the supper club before I got round to getting some baskets.

·   Ladles — buy some different-sized ones. We use one for the oils and we use one that's the perfect serving size so you only have to ladle once for the soups.

·   Ice cream scoops — you remember the ones they used at school to ball up the mash potatoes? Yep, those. We use a big one for the miso and a small one for the chilli paste, perfect portion control every time.

·   A microplane — definitely worth getting, you'll never look at a box grater again.

·   A large pair of chopsticks — something about the size of Harry Potter's wand, you'll use these to stir the noodles while they're boiling.

·   A sharp knife — it doesn't have to be fancy, I use a Japanese bread knife for just about everything in the kitchen.

index

thanks

Firstly, to my mum and dad Cynthia and Alistair for their continued love and support – from when I said I wanted to be a cook when I was 25, they told me to just go for it if that's what I wanted to do – I think they were just happy I'd finally found something I loved doing.

My sister Elena who loves what I do and at any opportunity shouts about me to whoever's listening. On a side note, my mum, dad and sister are all incredible cooks – better than me and I think that's where I got the bug from.

My brother-in-law Ned – another great cook and noodle soup fanatic.

Maria Georgiou – one of the greats, a friend 'til the end, thank you for everything.

Tamika Abaka-Wood – thank you for going out every Saturday night.

Toby Green – for everything you do day in and day out, relentlessly, always with a smile on your face, thanks for believing in me and deciding to go on this ride with me.

Jess Ebsworth for all your illustrations and branding since day one, Supa Ya would not be where it is without you. Huge thanks to you and Brian O'Tuama for designing the book – I'm so happy with it.

Sam Ashton, Giles Smith and Tom Welsh for the photography, your vision, creativity, sense of humour and playlists.

Kitty Coles for your unique eye on the food styling and recipe tweaks.

Rhiannon and Matthew Butler – two of my biggest cheerleaders.

Everyone at Pavilion and HarperCollins, especially Steph Milner for giving me this opportunity, Laura Russell for her insight and help, and Kiron Gill for putting it all together (sorry for all my annoying questions).

To everyone who's ever worked at Supa Ya past and present, with special shouts to Abel Wilson, Yota Kitade, Anna Makri, Catriona Poon, Isabella Duckworth Lima Pinto, Samuel Cooksley, Stefanel Tok, Lola Demille, Ezra Sartaj, Francis Joseph, Matthew Morishima, Holly Ayres, Kira Mckee and Adessa Simpson.

To everyone I've collabbed with and who has shouted about us since day one – Ed and Jaime at Four Legs, Chris Leach at Manteca, Ellen and Pete at Lucky & Joy, the whole team at Top Cuvée, Elliot at Eat Lagom, George Lamb and everyone at Wildfarmed, Ianthe Cox-Willmot, John Sunyer, Shaun Whitmore, Joe Grossman, Tommo Greer, Elly Barham Marsh, Suzie Bakos at Little Sauce, Emily Yeoh and Ana Da Costa at Two Hot Asians, Ixta Belfrage, Jenny Phung at Ling Ling's, Spasia Dinkovski at Mystic Borek, Megan Moore, Lou Boxy, James Chant at Matsudai Ramen, Omar at Komugi, Neil Rankin, Freya Coote, James Moyle, Chris Shilling, Harry Jones, Jaime Taylor and to everyone who came to the supperclubs, pop-ups and all the customers who eat with us.

And lastly, to my good friend Hannell – thanks for going on holiday with me mate.

Pavilion
An imprint of HarperCollins Publishers Ltd
1 London Bridge Street
London SE1 9GF

www.harpercollins.co.uk

HarperCollins Publishers
Macken House
39/40 Mayor Street Upper
Dublin 1
D01 C9W8
Ireland

10 9 8 7 6 5 4 3 2 1

First published in Great Britain by Pavilion
An imprint of HarperCollins Publishers 2023

Copyright © Pavilion 2023
Text © Luke Findlay 2023

Luke Findlay asserts the moral right to be identified as the author of this work.
A catalogue record of this book is available from the British Library.

ISBN 978 0 00 860251 2

This book is produced from independently certified FSC™ paper to ensure responsible forest management.

For more information visit: www.harpercollins.co.uk/green

Publishing Director: Stephanie Milner
Commissioning Editor: Kiron Gill
Editor: Kate Reeves Brown
Editorial Assistant: Shamar Gunning
Design Director: Laura Russell
Designer: Brian O'Tuama
Layout Designer: James Boast
Senior Production Controller: Grace O'Byrne
Photography: Sam Ashton
Photography Assistants: Giles Smith and Tom Welsh
Photography Studio: Studio Sachet
Food Stylist: Kitty Coles
Prop Stylist: Rachel Vere
Illustrator: Jess Ebsworth
Proofreader: John Friend
Indexer: Hilary Bird

Printed in Malaysia

All rights reserved. No part of this publication may be reproduced, stored in a retrieval system, or transmitted, in any form or by any means, electronic, mechanical, photocopying, recording or otherwise, without the prior written permission of the publishers.

This book is sold subject to the condition that it shall not, by way of trade or otherwise, be lent, re sold, hired out or otherwise circulated without the publisher's prior consent in any form of binding or cover other than which it is published and without a similar condition including this condition being imposed on the subsequent purchaser.